~SPURGEON~

Grace Abounding in a Believer's Life

~ ~

CHARLES SPURGEON
CHRISTIAN LIVING CLASSICS

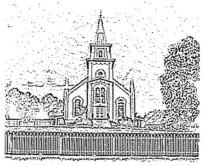

CHARLES SPURGEON
Christian Living Classics

Grace Abounding in a Believer's Life

Compiled and Edited by ROBERT HALL

Emerald Books

P.O. Box 635 • Lynnwood, Washington 98046

Scripture quotations are taken from the King James Version of the Bible

Grace Abounding in a Believer's Life
Copyright © 1994
Lance C. Wubbels

Published by Emerald Books
P.O. Box 635
Lynnwood, WA 98046

ISBN 1-883002-09-5

Printed in the United States of America

About the Editor

ROBERT HALL is the pseudonym for Lance Wubbels, the managing editor of Bethany House Publishers. His interest in the writings of Charles Spurgeon began while doing research on an editorial project that required extensive reading of Spurgeon's sermons. He discovered a wealth of sermon classics that are filled with practical, biblical insight for every believer and written in a timeless manner that makes them as relevant today as the day they were spoken. His desire is to select and present Spurgeon's writings in a way that will appeal to a wide audience of readers and allow one of the greatest preachers of all time to enrich believers' lives.

About the Author

CHARLES HADDON SPURGEON (1834–1892) was the remarkable British "Boy Preacher of the Fens" who became one of the truly greatest preachers of all time. Coming from a flourishing country pastorate in 1854, he accepted a call to pastor London's New Park Street Chapel. This building soon proved too small and so work on Spurgeon's Metropolitan Tabernacle was begun in 1859. Meanwhile his weekly sermons were being printed and having a remarkable sale—25,000 copies every week in 1865 and translated into more than twenty languages.

Spurgeon built the Metropolitan Tabernacle into a congregation of over 6,000 and added well over 14,000 members during his thirty-eight-year London ministry. The combination of his clear voice, his mastery of language, his sure grasp of Scripture, and a deep love for Christ produced some of the noblest preaching of any age. An astounding 3,561 sermons have been preserved in sixty-three volumes, *The New Park Street Pulpit* and *The Metropolitan Tabernacle Pulpit*, from which the chapters of this book have been selected and edited.

During his lifetime, Spurgeon is estimated to have preached to 10,000,000 people. He remains history's most widely read preacher. There is more available material written by Spurgeon than by any other Christian author, living or dead. His sixty-three volumes of sermons stand as the largest set of books by a single author in the history of Christianity, comprising the equivalent to the twenty-seven volumes of the ninth edition of the *Encyclopedia Britannica*.

Contents

Introduction

THE EULOGIES OF CHARLES SPURGEON'S preaching are almost endless. It is a preaching legacy that can never be forgotten; it may never be surpassed. Considered by his peers then and now as "The Prince of Preachers," Charles Spurgeon will stand for many years to come as the epitome of pulpit mastery. Joseph Parker, another of London's famous preachers, wrote: "Mr. Spurgeon's career has proved that evangelical teaching can draw around itself the greatest congregation in the world, and hold it for a lifetime. . . . The great voice has ceased. It was the mightiest voice I ever heard."

Spurgeon built London's Metropolitan Tabernacle into the world's largest independent congregation during the nineteenth century. During his remarkable thirty-eight-year ministry, his passionate biblical expositing transformed the lives of thousands of listeners as he addressed the deepest needs of the human heart. And at the core of Spurgeon's message was always the abounding grace of God. It was the central doctrine around which his message and ministry focused. A sample of what he said gives a sense of the inspiration that Spurgeon drew from it:

> The mercy of God's heart means His hearty mercy, His cordial delight in mercy. Remission of sins is a business into which the Lord throws His heart. He forgives with an intensity of will and readiness of soul. God made heaven and earth with His fingers, but He gave His Son with His heart so that He might save sinners. The Eternal God has thrown His

whole soul into the business of redeeming men. If you desire to see God most godlike, it is in the pardon of men's sin. If you desire to read the character of God written out in capital letters, you must study the visitation of His love in the person of His dear Son and all the wonderful works of infinite grace that spring from Him. It is a grand sight to behold!

Yes, the grace of God is amazing to behold and seems so simple. "Grace be to you and peace from God the Father, and from our Lord Jesus Christ" was the apostolic blessing that was repeated throughout the epistles and has stood throughout the centuries as the fundamental heartbeat of the Christian gospel. Grace is the undeserved, unmerited favor of God, which alone cleanses a sinner from sin and guilt. Grace tells a man that, in spite of all that is true about him, God still looks on him with love.

Yet, history has proven, and personal Christian experience proves, that the grace of God often falls prey to religious legalism. As one of the church's greatest statesmen regarding the role of grace in a believer's life, Martin Luther's words are insightful: "The article of justification is fragile. Not in itself, of course, but in us. I know how quickly a person can forget the joy of the Gospel. I know in what slippery places even those who seem to have a good footing in the matter of faith, in the midst of the conflict when we should be consoling ourselves with the gospel, the law rears up and begins to rage all over our conscience. I say the gospel is frail because we are frail."

When Luther and the European Reformers carried the torch of freedom against the legalists of their day, grace was the battle cry. They were hated by the church and called heretics. When the eighteenth- and early nineteenth-century revival spread across Great Britain and into America, it was grace again that led the way through the mighty preaching of Wesley, Edwards, Whitefield, and other spokesmen for God.

In our own era, the need of the message of grace is just as pressing. Charles Swindoll, one of the great Christian leaders of our day writes:

Scarcely a day passes when I am not reminded of the need for a book emphasizing the full extent of grace, giving people permission to be free, absolutely free in Christ. Why? Because so few are! Bound and shackled by legalists' lists of do's and don'ts, intimidated and immobilized by others' demands and expectations, far too many in God's family merely exist in the tight radius of bondage, dictated by those who have appointed themselves our judge and jury. Long enough have we lived like frightened deer in a restrictive thicket of negative regulations. Long enough have we submitted to the do's and don'ts of religious kings of the mountain. Long enough have we been asleep while all around us the grace killers do their sinister nighttime work. No longer! It's time to awaken. The dawn is bright with grace.

I trust that this outstanding volume of messages from Charles Spurgeon will do for you exactly what Swindoll desires: it will give you permission to be free, absolutely free in Christ. The grace that calls a man to follow Jesus Christ costs the man his life, but it gives him the only true life. It is the door to discipleship and joy for which Christ gave His life on the cross. What a tragedy to not experience the grace of God in its fullness or to experience it only in a measure.

I invite you to read these twelve select chapters on faith as you would listen to a trusted and skilled pastor, for that is what Spurgeon was. There is nothing speculative about Spurgeon's teaching; just the rock-solid truth. Spurgeon will meet you where you live, and you will not be disappointed.

Careful editing has helped to sharpen the focus of these sermons while retaining the authentic and timeless flavor they undoubtedly bring.

God gives His grace in the most emphatic sense. He is not compelled to be gracious by the force of our demands, but He often gives to those who have never asked of Him: "I am found of them that sought me not" (Isa. 65:1). He calls by His divine power those who before were unwilling to come to Him. Think of the case of Saul of Tarsus who received light and grace when he was in the act of persecuting the saints. God gives His grace as freely as the sun showers the earth with sunlight. See how freely the sun visits the tiny flower that holds up its cup to have it filled with sunshine! How it peers into the glade of the forest where by the brook the fern loves the shade. Whether the lark flies up to meet it or the mole burrows in the earth to escape its light, the sun shines all the same. It fills the heavens and floods the earth with the brilliance that it is its nature to diffuse. The Lord comes by promise to those who seek Him, but He comes also in sovereign grace to those who do not seek Him.

Chapter One

Grace for Grace

Now we have received, not the spirit of the world, but the spirit which is of God; that we might know the things that are freely given to us of God—1 Corinthians 2:12.

THE COURSE OF OUR FALLEN RACE has been a succession of failures. Whenever there has been an apparent rise, it has been followed by a real fall. Into ever-increasing darkness the human mind seems resolved to plunge itself in its struggles after a false light. When men have been fools, they have danced in a delirium of sin. When men have been sober, they have given themselves to a phantom wisdom of their own that has revealed their folly more than ever. The story of mankind is a sad tale! Read it in the light of God's Word, and it will bring tears to your very heart.

The only hope for man was that God should intervene, and He has as though He began a new creation or wrought a resurrection out of the kingdom of death. God has come into human history, and here the bright lights begin. Where God is at work in grace, abounding sin is conquered, hope begins, and good becomes a reality. This is always markedly the effect of a break in the natural course of things, a supernatural product that would never have been in this poor world had it been left alone. Humanity left to itself is like an avalanche rushing down the steep mountainside. Lo, God in Christ Jesus throws Himself in the way, intervening so as to be crushed beneath the descending rocks. But He rises from the dreadful burial, stops the terrible avalanche, hurls back the tremendous mass, and changes the whole aspect of history. In this divine intervention we behold and adore the almighty grace of God.

In the intervention of omnipotent grace, we note that the Lord so works as to preserve His own glory. He takes care that no flesh shall glory in His presence. He might have used the power of His might, but He has not. He might have instructed man by man's own wisdom, but He has not. He might have declared His gospel with the excellency of human speech, but He has not. He has refused the armor of a king and taken for His only tool the sling of a shepherd. He has placed His treasure of truth not in the golden vase of talent but in the earthen vessels of lowly minds. He has made men speak for Him not under the spell of genius but as they have been moved by His Holy Spirit. The Lord of hosts will save men, but He will not give men a yard of space for boasting. He will grant them a salvation that shall humble them in the dust and lead them to know that He is God and beside Him there is none else. "The LORD of hosts hath purposed it, to stain the pride of all glory, and to bring into contempt all the honourable of the earth" (Isa. 23:9). God's gracious intervention reveals His sovereignty, His wisdom, His power, His love, and His grace, but it reveals nothing in men that can admit a boastful thought.

The Lord has worked in a way consistent with His central intervention that was seen at the cross, where Jesus unveiled Jehovah's way of revealing power in weakness. It was in this connection that Paul says, "For I determined not to know any thing among you, save Jesus Christ, and him crucified" (1 Cor. 2:2). He knew that there was nothing else to know. The plan of the cross is to conquer death by death, to remove sin by the endurance of the penalty, to work mightily by suffering terribly, to glorify Himself through shame. The cross where Christ died was the abyss of reproach and the climax of suffering, but it was also the focus of God's intervening grace. He there glorified Himself with shame and death, not with honor and power. The great self-sacrifice of God is the great victory of grace. It is most sweet to think that all the ways of God to men are in harmony with this way of the cross and that the cross is the pattern of the Lord's constant method of accomplishing His designs of grace rather by weakness than by strength, by suffering rather than by the splendor of His majesty.

Let me add that this way that God has taken is entirely suitable to the condition of those whom He saves. If salvation had been by human excellence, I could never have been saved. If the plan of salvation had required that in which a man might rightly glory, how could it have come to sinners without strength or goodness? Such a gospel would have been no gospel to us, for it would have been out of our reach. God's plans are workable plans, suitable to the weakness of our fallen race. In Christ He comes to the wounded man where he is and does not ask him to come a certain part of the way in his fainting condition.

It is my delightful task to set before you the exceeding freeness of the grace of God, which is an open door that you may enter boldly. The verse we will study from First Corinthians speaks of the gifts of God freely given to us, of the way by which we may receive them, and of how we come to know their excellence and value. In all these three things it shows us that everything is of grace—it is given of grace, it is received through grace, and it is understood by grace. "Grace reigns," and grace alone.

The Things of God Are Freely Given

All the blessings of salvation are a gift. All that comes by our Lord Jesus to save and sanctify men is a gift. We are not asked, in any sense, to bring a price to God whereby to purchase our pardon, justification, or eternal life. Where the notion of purchase is for an instant hinted at, it is only to show plainly how free the blessing is: "come ye, buy, and eat; yea, come, buy wine and milk without money and without price" (Isa. 55:1). God freely gives His grace, expecting nothing in return, but that we do as freely receive as He does freely bestow. Do not reach into your bank account, for money is useless as to purchasing salvation. Give up on searching in your character or in your resolutions for some little recommendation. Neither the coin of the rich nor that of the self-righteous is currency here. The free grace of God would be insulted by being put up to auction or set forth to sale. "The gift of God is eternal life though Jesus Christ our Lord" (Rom. 6:23).

It is a gift and not a prize. There are heavenly prizes to run for, to be fought for, and to be obtained through divine help. There is a recompense of reward to which we are to look and a crown for which we are to strive, but the grace that forgives sin and works faith is no prize for exertion but a gift to those without strength. "So then it is not of him that willeth, nor of him that runneth, but of God that sheweth mercy" (Rom. 9:16). Jehovah will have mercy on whom He will have mercy according to the good pleasure of His will. Salvation is not granted to men as the result of anything they are, or do, or resolve to be, but is the undeserved gift of heaven. If it were of works, it would not be of grace; but it is of faith, that it might be of grace alone.

The blessings of salvation are freely *given* to us by God; therefore, they are not a temporary loan that is one day to be recalled. Our heavenly heritage is not held on lease or upon terms of annual payment. It is an unencumbered freehold to every man that has by faith put his foot upon it. When God has given salvation, the deed is done and can never be reversed. If your sin has been blotted out, it can never be written again! God has declared that He has forgiven our transgression, and then He adds, "Their sins and iniquities will I remember no more" (Heb. 10:17). There is no playing fast and loose in connection with the everlasting love of God and its glorious acts. If you have God, you have Him by an eternal holding that none can deprive you of. The things of God are all free gifts without legal conditions appended to them that make their tenure one of payment rather than of absolute gift. The blessings of pardon, justification, and eternal life are gifts without an "if" in the core of them, rendering them uncertain. No, the gift of God is "eternal life."

Saving blessings are gifts *of God*. Every part of salvation is to the highest degree precious, for it is of God. It is the gift of the heavenly King, the gift of the Almighty Sovereign, whose hand makes the gift priceless. That which your father gave you, preserve, for there is a sanctity in the gift of love. But that which your God has given you, prize above all else. His touch has perfumed the gift with unutterable fragrance. Value every part of the work of grace because it came from God and leads to God. God's gifts are always worthy of the giver. His gifts are solid gold and lasting treasure. The gifts of divine grace have a quality of divinity about them. His grace is like the rest of His nature. How you are blessed if you are divinely pardoned and justified! "It is God that justifieth! Who is he that condemneth?" (Rom. 8:33–34). Jehovah is your strength and song; He also has become your salvation.

I like to think of every blessing of grace that I have received as coming from God because each mercy then becomes prophetic of more. God is unchangeable, and therefore what He has given He will give again. The stream that has begun to flow will never cease flowing. The more the Lord gives, the more we may expect. Each mercy as it comes makes room for another larger than itself, even as the narrow end of the wedge opens the way for its wider portion. John Bunyan said that God's flowers bloom double: not only do they bloom double, but they bloom sevenfold. Therefore be encouraged. The least of the things that are freely given to us by God draws behind it an endless chain of more than golden links of love. The seed of salvation, glory, and eternal life is small as a grain of mustard seed, but he who has it has received what neither earth nor heaven can fully contain. What a mercy is a single mercy!

Think of that word *freely*: "the things that are *freely given* to us of God." These are sweet words to those who have not yet found grace and music to those who have found it and are enjoying it. Surely it would have been enough to say "given," but the additional "freely" is meant to make the meaning doubly plain. When we say "grace," there is no need to say *free* grace, is there? Yet there are some people who will be conveniently deaf, if they can. It is written so no one can misunderstand, even if they try.

How is salvation freely given? It comes from God *without compulsion*. No one can force mercy from God, and blessed be

His name, there is no need to think of such a thing. God gives so freely that it is *without persuasion*. God was never persuaded to be gracious. He is ready to pardon, and His grace persuades us to accept mercy. Our praying does not turn the heart of God to love us but proves that we are turning to love Him. You have not to convert an unwilling God to be willing to forgive. The conversion is in *your* will, not in His will: "he delighteth in mercy" (Mic. 7:18). The fountain of divine love pours forth its streams of grace at all seasons without pressure. There is no need to tread the grapes of mercy to force forth their wonderful juice.

The grace of God is so free in its gifts that the gifts come *without suggestion*. A man may be generous, yet he may need to be reminded to help the needy. No one has prompted the grace of God. Out of His own heart the thought has come by itself. The gifts of His grace were in His eternal purpose from of old, and there of His good pleasure. He freely instructs us how to pray for those gifts that He has of old purposed to bestow. Our prayer only shows that He has instructed us. He gives freely in the sense of absolute spontaneousness.

He also gives *without grudging*. We hear men say, "Well, I suppose I must give something." They give as if they are parting with blood. A man's fingers may tremble and linger long over the coin that has to be extracted as forcibly as if it were a tooth. One wonders if the coin's image is left upon the man's fingers when the coin has been held with such pressure. But the Lord gives out of the greatness of His heart without a trace of unwillingness. Even the priceless gift of His Son was *freely* given. There is never a grudge in the Lord's mind toward those who draw upon Him the most largely and the most frequently. "Let him ask of God, that giveth to all men liberally, and upbraideth not" (James 1:5). Many who give to others take the opportunity to first upbraid, saying, "You must have been wasteful and lazy to require my help." God gives liberally and adds no sorrow with it to those who humbly seek at His hands. Oh, the splendor of the generosity of God! He is ready to save, to deliver, to bestow His goodness. The cost was paid long ago on Calvary's tree, and that is over. All that comes is freely given.

We use the word *freely* in the sense of bountifully. Free grace does not limit itself by calculation and is not bound by applicant to estimates. The Lord provides more than need demands. The mere crumbs from the Lord's table would suffice to feed the multitudes. The Lord does not give His Spirit by measure (John 3:34). The more grace you can take in, the better pleased the Lord will be with you. Your capacity will fail long before the provisions end. The Lord desires you to open your mouth wide, and He will fill it (Ps. 81:10). It is easier for Him to give than for you to open your mouth. He encourages and requests you to bring large petitions with you when you come before His mercy seat. Come and receive "the things that are freely given to us of God."

God gives His grace in the most emphatic sense. He is not compelled to be gracious by the force of our demands, but He often gives to those who have never asked of Him: "I am found of them that sought me not" (Isa. 65:1). He calls by His divine power those who before were unwilling to come to Him. Think of the case of Saul of Tarsus who received light and grace when he was in the act of persecuting the saints. God gives His grace as freely as the sun showers the earth with sunlight. See how freely the sun visits the tiny flower that holds up its cup to have it filled with sunshine! How it peers into the glade of the forest where by the brook the fern loves the shade. Whether the lark flies up to meet it or the mole burrows in the earth to escape its light, the sun shines all the same. It fills the heavens and floods the earth with the brilliance that it is its nature to diffuse. The Lord comes by promise to those who seek Him, but He comes also in sovereign grace to those who do not seek Him.

Now what are these things that are freely given to us by God? *They are altogether immeasurable.* Shall I tell you what they are in one word? GOD. God gives us God. *God the Father gives Himself* to the unworthy sons of men. He becomes their Father and their friend. He gives them His wisdom, His power, His love, His immutability. He gives Himself to them to be their possession forever. In adoption He gives His fatherhood and grants them sonship, so that they may cry, "Our Father, which art in heaven." He gives pardon and acceptance. He grants them answers to their prayers in ten thousand ways. He gives them His Providence to guide and lead them. He gives them all they need for this life, and then He gives them an inheritance with Himself forever in the world to come. He who gave us Jesus also gives us freely all things (Rom. 8:32).

The Son of God also gives Himself. "Who loved me, and gave himself for me" (Gal. 2:20). "Who his own self bare our sins in his own body on the tree" (1 Pet. 2:24). Jesus gives His people His blood to wash out their sins, His righteousness to cover them with beauty, His intercession to plead their cause, and His enthronement to secure their victory. He gives His loving care to prepare a place for them in the sky. He gives His resurrection to bring them up from the grave, and His union with them to preserve them through the perils of life. We are married to Him, and so He freely gives His heart's love to us. Even His crown, His throne, and His heaven He freely gives to His chosen. What a gift of grace! "For God so loved the world, that he gave his only begotten Son" (John 3:16). He is God's unspeakable gift!

The Holy Spirit also freely gives Himself to us. He is the free Spirit (Ps. 51:12), and never freer than when He gives Himself to enlighten, quicken, convert, comfort, and sanctify His people. He leads to repentance and faith. He conducts to knowledge and holiness. He preserves and perfectly conforms us to the image of Christ.

All things are yours, the free gifts of God. Now if the Apostle Paul could speak of these things as free gifts, you and I may well be glad to accept these priceless treasures on the same terms. It may be simple language, but the message is sublime!

The Power to Receive These Gifts Is Also Freely Given

So how do we make these blessings our own? The text says, "we have received ... the spirit which is of God." The power with which we receive these gifts is the power of the Holy Ghost. And this, also, we do not purchase or deserve, but freely receive.

The power to grasp Christ does not lie in our nature in its own strength or goodness. Our state is that of death, and death cannot grasp life. God the Holy Spirit must breathe life into us before we can rise from the grave of our natural depravity and lay hold upon Christ. "The natural man receiveth not the things of the Spirit of God" (1 Cor. 2:14). It is not in unrenewed human nature to even see the kingdom of God.

The power to receive the things of God lies not in high gifts or attainments. Genius is no help toward grace. Indeed, great talent and great learning often miss the way where lowliness travels with ease. Paul makes a great point of this: "For ye see your calling, brethren, how that not many wise men after the flesh, not many mighty, not many noble, are called" (1 Cor. 1:26). The power to receive the blessings of God does not lie in talent at all, but it lies in the Spirit of God. You think that if you had a long hand you could reach the grace of God. No, but if you have a withered hand, that grace can reach you. Grace is not tied to the rare gifts of genius or to the precious acquirements of experience or to the high attainments of learning. The power to receive is still of the Holy Spirit, and the Holy Spirit does not find good in us but brings it to us. A person may suffer greatly from a sense of guilt and the fear of punishment before he lays hold of Christ, but that did not earn him Christ. The wounded man is not restored by his pains, and the starving man is not fed by his hunger. The power to lay hold of Christ is a spiritual power that must be given from above. No process of discipline or education or evolution can enable a man to lay hold of the things of God. The man must be born again from above, and His heart must be opened to receive the grace of God.

The receptive power is *not bestowed by human excitement* or by the oratorical power of the preacher to whom the man listens. Put the thought away that if you could just hear a certain preacher, you could believe. You will never believe in Him if you are looking to yourself or someone else for the power to believe. It is the truth itself and the Spirit who can make the truth clear to you that will lead you to see how worthy your Savior is of your confidence. The Holy Spirit can enable you to receive all the gifts of God. You will feel the soft, sweet influence of repentance melting you to tears on account of sin. You will feel something telling you that in Christ there is just what you want, and you will feel a resolve forming in your heart: "I will have it if it may be had." Then you will come to a solemn decision for the present hour: "I will have it *now*. I will turn my eyes to the cross and look to Him who hung upon it and trust my soul's weight on Him." You may not know at the time that the moving power is the Holy Spirit, but no one else works this in us but the Holy Ghost. We may not hear the Spirit's voice or recognize His person at the time, but being emptied of self and being led to accept the things that are freely given to us of God are clearly the work of God.

Remember that there is the Spirit of God and the spirit of the world. The spirit of the world is everywhere active and works evil against believers. Only the Spirit of God can save you. The spirit of the world will ruin all who yield to it. Keep as clear of the spirit of the world as possible, for its pestilential influence will injure you. Be aware that the religious world is more dangerous by far than the sensual world. Men profess religion and yet cunningly undermine it. Religion wears the sheepskin but has all the fierceness of the wolf. Do not meddle with that which is doubtful. If you would find eternal life, go where the Spirit of God works. Search the Scriptures and hear the truth through which the Holy Spirit usually operates. And associate with those in whom the Spirit of God dwells. Hear the preaching and teaching that come from God, for they alone lead you to Him. Take heed of those who profess godliness but are tainted with the spirit of the world. Follow the right Spirit, for in so doing you will find the things of God.

Do you see how free salvation is? Not only are the gifts of grace most free but the very hand with which we take the gift is nerved to do so by God's grace. God gives not only the blessing to the heart but also the heart to receive the blessing.

The Knowledge of These Gifts Is Freely Given

A knowledge of the things freely given of God is communicated to our minds by the revelation contained in the inspired Scriptures. These sacred writings are open to all, and all are invited to search them. Read the Word of God, and you will know in the letter what are the free gifts of God to men. But this saving knowledge is not received by simply reading or being taught the truth. The head learns by nature, but the heart must learn by grace. The way to know the things of God is for that which is written in God's Word to be also written upon the heart by the same Spirit who wrote in the book. It requires the appropriation of faith to give an apprehension to the understanding. An experimental enjoyment creates true acquaintance. Go to the Holy Spirit and ask Him to enable you to take the things that God freely gives.

If you desire to know more of the infinite preciousness of the gifts of God, it is a wise ambition. It will be fully and freely satisfied by the Holy Spirit. Go to Him, for He is the greatest Teacher. His knowledge surpasses all other, for He knows the mind of God. No man can communicate to you what he does not know, and no man knows the mind of God but the Spirit of God. The mind and meaning of God in every gift of grace the Spirit can unfold to you. No one is being taught effectually unless he is taught of the Spirit. All other teaching is superficial and therefore temporary and vain. But the Holy Spirit speaks to the soul and writes lines of truth on the fleshly tablets of the heart so that they can never be erased. Only the Holy Spirit can lead you into the inner secret of the sacred treasure house.

By the same divine aid you must be enabled to feed upon these choice things and to have a full enjoyment of them. The things of God are best known by a personal enjoyment of them. When you feed upon a Scripture and extract the juice from a divine promise, then the Lord has made you freely to know the blessings of His covenant. May the Holy Spirit enlighten your eyes and nourish your heart to see the mercy seat and all the glory of the Lord your God!

Go to this high school of heaven. The terms are "nothing to pay," though the education is beyond all others. It is a blessed school wherein sinners are made saints and saints are made to grow into the likeness of Jesus. Eternal life is the gift of God in its first breathing, and it is still the gift of God in its highest development. When you stand before the throne of the Most High, you will stand there through grace alone. All the way from sin's pit to heaven's gate the whole road is paved with grace. We do not at first freely receive and then afterwards have to live upon hard-earned wages. No. Still He works in us to will and to do, and we lovingly work under His divine guidance as we are strengthened by His divine power (Phil. 2:12–13).

Learn from these things to *be humble*. If you know anything, you have been taught it. If you possess anything, it has been given to you. You are a charity child. A proud saint is a contradiction in terms. "God resisteth the proud, but giveth grace unto the humble" (James 4:6).

In the next place, *be generous*. I cannot believe in a stingy saint. Here again is a flat contradiction in terms. "Freely ye have received, freely give" (Matt. 10:8). He who turns over the coin in his pocket to make it as small as ever he can before he gives it is a poor creature. The child of God should be free-hearted. He should give himself away because Jesus gave Himself for us. You should be large of heart, for you serve a large-hearted Christ.

Next, *be ready to impart what you know*. If the Spirit of God has made you to know the things freely given of God, try to tell someone else. Don't act is if you had a patent or a monopoly and wanted grace to be a secret. You do not have the gift of God if you have no desire that others should have it. If you have no wish to bring others to heaven, you are not going there yourself.

Try to impart this knowledge in the way in which you received it: by the Holy Spirit. Then go and teach it in the power of the Spirit of God. Look not to the power of man's knowledge, eloquence, or experience, but look to the guidance of the Spirit. Better five words in the spirit than a long oration in your own power.

If the Lord has give us all these things freely, *let us praise Him*. It is good to let the living water of praise burst the pipes and flood the streets. Why make it so difficult for the Lord to pull at the rope before our bells speak? Let us praise Him for the riches of His grace!

Grace has been displayed of ancient times in the great council chamber where all the attributes of God sat in solemn conclave to devise a way by which God should be glorified. Foreknowledge, as one of the attributes of God, prophesied that man, if made fallible, would sadly fall. Justice, therefore, arose and thundered forth His word that if man fell, he must be punished. Grace, however, asked whether it could not be possible that man should be saved and yet justice should be satisfied. Infinite Wisdom answered the question, and God's own Son was the answer. He promised that in the fullness of time, He would become a son for us and bear the whole weight of Jehovah's justly merited wrath as our redemption. Now while all the other attributes displayed themselves in the council chamber, when our reverent soul dares venture into that once secret but now revealed will of the Most High, we are compelled to admire all the attributes of God but most of all His grace. It seems to me that grace presided at this meeting, that grace pressed man's redemption, that grace inspired wisdom, that grace defended man when justice might have spoken against him. Grace was our advocate. Christ Jesus, who is grace Himself, long ago stood as the Wonderful, the Counselor, and devised the plan, pleaded our cause, and promised to work it out. The glory of grace as it sits with its crown upon its head in the council chamber of eternity is a subject worthy of your devout reflection and quiet meditation.

Chapter Two

The Glory of Grace

The glory of his grace—Ephesians 1:6.

GOD IS ESSENTIALLY GLORIOUS. Even were there no eyes to behold Him, no lips to declare His praise, no intelligent creatures to obey Him, He would be infinitely glorious in Himself. Nevertheless, God has chosen to exhibit His glory that He may receive praise out of the hearts of intelligent beings, who, beholding the varied and wonderful manifestations of the exceeding riches of His grace, may be compelled to glorify Him with joy and gratitude. It is also in this sense of glory being given to God that He is glorious. He is admired, He is beloved, He is adored.

Every attribute of God has its glory, not only in its essence but also through its exhibition of Himself. God's power is glorious in the works of His hands. His skill, His wisdom, His benevolence—all these are to be seen in those works of nature that meet our eyes every day. God's justice is glorious, and we sometimes tremble to think how awfully glorious it is in the lowest pit of hell. But my purpose here is to isolate "the glory of his grace." God's grace is in itself glorious and really brings glory to all the other attributes. When God glorifies His grace, He glorifies His whole character. Grace becomes a platform upon which all the perfections of Deity exhibit themselves. Grace becomes a light that shines upon all the rest, and they, though bright enough in themselves, seem to be doubly bright when they glow in its brilliance.

The Glory of Divine Grace As It Has Been Displayed

Grace has been displayed of ancient times *in the great council chamber* where all the attributes of God sat in solemn conclave to devise a way by which God should be glorified. Foreknowledge, as one of the attributes of God, prophesied that man, if made fallible, would sadly fall. Justice, therefore, arose and thundered forth His word that if man fell, he must be punished. Grace, however, asked whether it could not be possible that man should be saved and yet justice should be satisfied. Infinite Wisdom answered the question, and God's own Son was the answer. He promised that in the fullness of time, He would become a son for us and bear the whole weight of Jehovah's justly merited wrath as our redemption. Now while all the other attributes displayed themselves in the council chamber, when our reverent soul dares venture into that once secret but now revealed will of the Most High, we are compelled to admire all the attributes of God but most of all His grace. It seems to me that grace presided at this meeting, that grace pressed man's redemption, that grace inspired wisdom, that grace defended man when justice might have spoken against him. Grace was our advocate. Christ Jesus, who is grace Himself, long ago stood as the Wonderful, the Counselor, and devised the plan, pleaded our cause, and promised to work it out. The glory of grace as it sits with its crown upon its head in the council chamber of eternity is a subject worthy of your devout reflection and quiet meditation.

Now the council is over, and grace steps forth to be glorified in another manner. Now, *it glorifies itself in its gifts.* See how grace gives to man blessings countless in number and priceless in value, scattering them along his pathway as if they were but stones. Yet every one is so precious that heaven itself can alone tell its worth. Finally, after having given man blessings through long ages, grace comes up to Calvary and there gives its all, its grandest gift. Grace gives up the incarnate Son of God to die. He gives up His own life and bows His head upon the cross. There may be much of shame and ignominy about the cross, but how much there is of glory and of majesty! There we see grace in the heart of Christ leading Him to save others while Himself He cannot save. We speak casually of these matters today, but the angels have never so spoken concerning grace glorified in the person of the dying Son of God. We did not think so slightly of grace when, for the first time, we saw Him to be ours in the day of our salvation. Neither will we when we see His face unveiled in heaven. Then we shall know what wondrous grace that was that made the glorious face become marred with sorrow and bowed that glorious head divine to the depths of the grave. Grace in its highest form is to be seen best on Calvary, but I think it is rather to be seen and felt than to be discussed. My feeble pen declines to bear the burden of a theme so weighty. I cannot stretch the wings of my imagination and rise to the height of this grand argument. I cannot adequately declare the praises of that grace seen in the dying Son of God on Calvary.

Since then you have had to glorify grace in its continued gifts. You have found that "He that spared not his own Son, but delivered him up for us all, how shall he not with him also freely give us all things?" (Rom. 8:32). What debtors we are! We are sunken fathoms deep in an ocean of indebtedness to God. Take out your pen and quickly write down all that He has given you. You may sit down quickly, but you will not rise speedily, for the full account could never be written. There are no scales to weigh these ponderous blessings. Earth has no coin by which to represent their value. We must get into the inconceivable before we can estimate the infinite, the unutterable value of those gifts that Jesus Christ continually gives to us by His grace outpoured.

Let us also speak of *grace in its triumphs* as we speak of "the glory of his grace." It is a strange thing that love should be a warrior and that grace should fight, but when grace came to make us gracious it found us graceless. The door was shut when Jesus came, though the man's hand and heart were open. Jesus Himself burst open the door and stormed the passage into the hearts of men. When mercy comes to bless, it finds us bent to the curse. We reject the mercy, and grace must overcome the will. It is only when man's graceless will is bound by fetters of sovereign grace that he is gracious at all. If there is such a thing as free will, Luther truly hit the mark when he called free will a slave. It is only our will in bonds that is truly free. When our will is constrained, it ranges at liberty. When grace binds it, then and only then is it free.

Think of the battles that grace has had with men, and what glory it has gained! In your case and mine, how stern has been the fight! Surely you recall the days when Jesus met you on the road and called to you in His love, but you spat in His face and passed Him by, making jest of the Crucified. Do you remember another time when He sent His dark messengers of sickness and sorrow, and you lay upon your bed. Jesus came to you again, and you uttered words to Him that looked like truth, but they were lying, deceptive words. You turned your face to the wall and vowed repentance, but you did not repent, sending Him on His way. You have never treated a friend as badly as you have treated Him. But grace has overcome you and made you a captive. The man may kick and struggle, but that man in God's time shall be arrested by the strong hand of sovereign grace and be transformed into a new man in Christ Jesus.

As we speak of the triumphs of grace, we must not forget the multitudes of triumphs grace has had in each soul. If you could bear in your body a mark for every triumph that grace has had in you, and if every mark were a jewel, would you not be covered from head to foot? Then consider that it is not merely one man in whom grace has worked but the countless myriads of souls that grace has overcome. Grace has gone into every land and every sort of habitation, and it has won its trophies. What a glorious day it will be when Christ shall enter into heaven with all His blood-bought saints and shall cry, "Here am I, Father, and the children whom You have given to me. Here are the ones whom I have rescued from the jaws of the lion and from the paws of the bear. Not one of them is missing. I have triumphed over

all their foes, and I bring them safely to their promised rest."
What a glory of grace!

The glory of divine grace is to be seen more fully when the whole plan of grace shall be worked out. None of us have a very clear idea of what the full design of divine grace is. I see the present world continually go on in its wickedness. It seems to me that justice is rather magnified than grace, for multitudes are daily descending into hell. But there is a bright season ahead when the Messiah Prince shall stand a second time among the sons of men, and we shall see that God's grace is so wonderfully magnified that our little hearts have never thought of how grandly the scene shall end. Then shall the earth ring with His praise. Then shall myriads of men and women be made to know Him. Then shall they come and bow down before Him, and all people shall call Him blessed. Then the enormous multitudes shall swell the roll of those chosen ones to such a marvelous degree that "a great multitude, which no man could number, of all nations, and kindreds, and people, and tongues, stood before the throne, and before the Lamb" (Rev. 7:9). Though the gate was narrow and the road was straight, yet the numbers of the saved and the songs of heaven shall prevail over all the growlings of hell. We shall be raised up to everlasting life and more than perfection, for it is the very likeness of the Son of God that we shall be given.

The Qualities That Distinguish Grace

Grace is glorious if we consider *its antiquity.* Grace is not a new cloth put into an old garment. Grace is not an alteration that God made to His original plan. It is not some addition that God made because of an unplanned catastrophe. He foresaw the fall from all eternity, and every iota of the plan of grace was devised of old. Before the sun was created, and long before he had been swaddled in mists, before the stars had known their resting places and sent the rays of their light through the thick darkness, long before the mountains knew their places or the water was poured in his fountains, God had chosen His people, had set His heart of love upon them, and had devised His plan. The covenant of grace is older than the oldest of things. Anything created is but a newly born infant, however aged it may seem. Grace has the hoary age upon its head. Venerable for age is the grace of God, and the plan of grace is no new chapter of modern compiling, but it is old as God's own eternity. O grace! You are from everlasting to everlasting.

The glory of grace consists not only in its antiquity but also in *its immutability*. The grace of God has never changed. Many a mighty river has been dried up, and even the seas have changed. The sun alters and everything grows dim with age, but grace flows on as it did at first. Its stream is just as deep, and its current just as mighty. There is no failing in grace, any more than there is any failing in God. Grace runs in one direct stream, and it has never been made to wind about. The chosen vessels of mercy have been washed in that stream. It has not passed by a single one, nor has one more been washed by it than those chosen ones of old. Grace given today must never be permitted to be thought of as being taken away tomorrow. If grace would be given temporarily and then taken away, I cannot imagine a more awful malediction. I would sooner perish as that fallen angel, that great sinner, Satan, than as one whom God had loved, if He did not love me forever. Better for God to send no gospel if He did not send an everlasting one. To give grace and then take it away would be the most awful method of tantalizing that was ever known. The grace of God is greatly magnified in its immutability as well as its antiquity.

Grace also derives great glory from *its freeness*. The grace of God is as free as the air we breathe. If anyone asks me whether he may believe in Christ, my answer is not that he may but that he is commanded to do so. If it is the command of God that we believe on Jesus Christ whom He has sent, a man is guilty of sin every moment that he lives without faith in Christ. It is commanded of us; therefore we can clearly say we have a right to it, for any man has a right to obey a divine command. If we are commanded, we have a perfect right to come. He who commands us to come to the feast gives us the only permit we need in that very command. Oh, that men would believe in the freeness of divine grace!

I preach the sovereignty of divine grace and desire to preach it with reverence before God and with faithfulness to man. But the freeness of grace is not inconsistent with the sovereignty of it. While none ever drink of that sacred fountain but those whom God sweetly constrains to drink, if men do not drink, the fault lies with them, and their blood will be on their own head forever. For the gospel cries, "Come. . . . whosoever will, let him take the water of life freely" (Rev. 22:17). The grace of God is free. No preparation is required before you can receive it, for God gives it even to men who do not ask for it: "I am found of them that sought me not" (Isa. 65:1). You are commanded to come to Jesus just as you are. The only barrier between you and Christ is your own depraved heart. If once you have the will, if God gives you the will to go to Christ, there is nothing that can keep you back and nothing that should intimidate you from coming. One of the glories of grace is its freeness, but a great many cannot see it. God's sovereignty is not at odds with the freeness of grace.

The glory of free grace will be found in *its benevolence*. What harm has grace ever done? There is not a man in the universe who can blame grace for any hurt he has received by it. I love a gospel that hurts nobody. If no one was saved by it, at least no one can point the finger at the gospel and say, "That has destroyed me." Their destruction lies within themselves. Grace scatters mercies but never anything that is the reverse of good. Its path is that of a conqueror, but its garments are not stained with blood, except its own blood. It is true that grace marches over the world, beating down every high look and levelling every lofty thing. But that is a blessing. Better to be levelled by grace than to be exalted by pride. Grace is a continual gushing fountain of mercy. It is a stream that is ever clear and unmixed. It is as Milton says, "'Tis better still, and better still, and better still, in infinite progression."

Surely one of the greatest glories of divine grace shall be when we *see the face of God with acceptance*. There will be at least three wonders in heaven. The first wonder is that we shall see so many there that we did not expect to be there. The second wonder is that we should miss so many we did expect to see there. But the third wonder is the greatest of all—to see ourselves there! When

I hear people censuring and condemning their fellow believers because they are not perfect, I wonder if these people know that they are saved by grace and that they have nothing that they have not received. I think that if they knew how they received what they have, they would not be so hard with those who have not got the blessing. We actually should always feel ourselves to be veritable beggars. The more right we come to be, the less we feel ourselves to be. That big letter "I" is so large with us all, pride is so interwoven into our nature, that I am afraid we shall never get it pulled out until we lie still in death. But if there is anything that can cure it, it is the fact that it is all of grace. Heaven shall show us how gracious God has been to us, but on earth let us walk humbly with our God. Let us always be giving glory to Christ, waiting for and expecting that happy day when we shall glorify Him with all His saints—when He shall come in the glory of His Father and all His holy angels with Him.

Will we not sing if we once get across the Jordan? Oh, what leapings for joy! What shoutings! What praise! What thanksgiving! Are you saying, "Oh, what temptations I have to battle with! Would to God that I were at rest!" Your rest may be nearer than you think. None of us are sure how near we are to heaven. That trouble you are dreading may never come, that trial may never arrive, for Christ may come before and catch us up to dwell with Him. I shall soon be dying. Time quickly fades away. Speed on, O time! Roll on your wheels, and every year race on! The shorter the road, the sooner I shall be with Him. The nearer I am to Jordan, the nearer I am to Canaan. Farewell, manna of the wilderness! Farewell, you fiery serpents and Amalekites! My soul shall cross the Jordan soon. I shall see the face of Him whom, though I have not yet seen, I do unceasingly adore—in whom I have a heaven on earth, and with whom I shall have an everlasting blessedness in that day when He calls me home to Himself.

I want to bring out into prominence those few words: "the tender mercy of our God." To me they gleam with the soft radiant light as of those matchless pearls by which the gates of heaven are made. There is an exceeding melody to my ear as well as to my heart in that word "tender." "Mercy" is music, and "tender mercy" is the most exquisite form of it, especially to a broken heart. To one who is despondent and despairing, this word is life from the dead. A great sinner who is deeply bruised by the lashes of conscience will bend his ear this way and cry, "Let me hear again the sweet sound of these words, tender mercy." If you think of this tenderness in connection with God, it will strike you with wonder that one so great should be so tender. We tend to think of omnipotence as a crushing energy that can hardly take account of little, feeble, suffering things. Yet if you consider it, the surprise will disappear and you will see with a new wonder of admiration that it must be so. He that is truly great among men is tender because He is great in heart as well as in thought and strength. The truly great spirit is always gentle, and God is infinitely great and tender. We read of His gentleness and of His tenderness toward the children of men, and we see them displayed to the full in the gospel of our salvation.

Chapter Three

The Tender Mercy of Our God

To give knowledge of salvation unto his people by the remission of their sins, through the tender mercy of our God; whereby the dayspring from on high hath visited us, to give light to them that sit in darkness and in the shadow of death, to guide our feet into the way of peace—Luke 1:77–79.

OBSERVE HOW ZACHARIAS joyfully extolled the remission of sins as one of the most extraordinary proofs of the tender mercy of our God. Zacharias had been unable to speak for a season as a chastisement for his unbelief, and therefore he used his recovered speech to sing of pardoning mercy. No salvation is possible without forgiveness, and so Zacharias said, "To give knowledge of salvation unto his people by the remission of their sins." The Lord could not forgive them on the ground of justice, but He did so because of His tender mercy. He passes by the sin of His people because He delights in mercy. Because God is love and has a great tenderness toward the work of His hands, He looks with anxious care upon burdened sinners to see how He can turn away His wrath and restore them to favor. For this reason alone there is remission of sins. Forgiveness does not come to us through any merit of ours, present or foreseen, but comes only through the tender mercy of God and the marvelous visit of love that came from it. Behold God in Christ Jesus, and there we see Him as full of compassion.

I want to bring out into prominence those few words: *"the tender mercy of our God."* To me they gleam with the soft radiant light as of those matchless pearls by which the gates of heaven are made. There is an exceeding melody to my ear as well as to my heart in that word *tender.* "Mercy" is music, and "tender mercy" is the most exquisite form of it, especially to a broken heart. To one who is despondent and despairing, this word is life from the dead. A great sinner who is deeply bruised by the lashes of conscience will bend his ear this way and cry, "Let me hear again the sweet sound of these words, *tender mercy.*" If you think of this tenderness in connection with God, it will strike you with wonder that one so great should be so tender. We tend to think of omnipotence as a crushing energy that can hardly take account of little, feeble, suffering things. Yet if you consider it, the surprise will disappear and you will see with a new wonder of admiration that it must be so. He that is truly great among men is tender because He is great in heart as well as in thought and strength. The truly great spirit is always gentle, and God is infinitely great and tender. We read of His gentleness and of His tenderness toward the children of men, and we see them displayed to the full in the gospel of our salvation. Very conspicuous is this "tender mercy of our God."

The original word is: "the mercy of the heart of our God." The evangelists, though they wrote in Greek, carried with them into that language the idioms of the Hebrew tongue. So they do not use an adjective, as it would seem from our translation of *tender mercy.* But they say, mercy of the bowels or of the inwards or of the heart of God. "The mercy of the heart of God" is to be seen in the remission of sin and in the visitation of His love when He comes to us as "the dayspring from on high." Great is the tenderness of divine mercy.

I call your attention to the original reading because it seems to me to mean not only tenderness but also much more. The mercy of the heart of God is the mercy of His great tenderness, the mercy of His infinite gentleness and consideration. But other thoughts come from this expression, which means the mercy of God's very soul. The heart is the seat and center of life, and mercy is to God as to His own life. "For I have no pleasure in the death of him that dieth, saith the Lord GOD: wherefore turn yourselves, and live ye" (Ezek. 18:32). God is love itself. Mercy is of the divine essence. There is no God apart from His heart, and mercy lies in the heart of God. He has bound up His mercy with His existence. As surely as God lives, He will grant remission of sins to those who turn to Him.

The mercy of God's heart means His hearty mercy, His cordial delight in mercy. Remission of sins is a business into which the Lord throws His heart. He forgives with an intensity of will and readiness of soul. God made heaven and earth with His fingers, but He gave His Son with His heart so that He might save sinners. The Eternal God has thrown His whole soul into the business of redeeming men. If you desire to see God most godlike, it is in the pardon of men's sin. If you desire to read the character of God written out in capital letters, you must study the visitation of His love in the person of His dear Son and all the wonderful works of infinite grace that spring from Him. It is a grand sight to behold God in earnest when He says, "Now will I arise" (Ps. 12:5). With awe we watch Him as He lays bare His arm, but this full energy of power is best seen when His work is grace. When He stirs up His strength to come and save us and brings the essence of His being into intense action to bless us, we are favored indeed. It is this watching to do us good, this eagerness to bless us, that is meant by the mercy of His heart. It is not only tenderness but also intensity, heartiness, eagerness, delight, and concentration of power. All this is to be seen in the dealing of God with guilty men when He visits them to grant them salvation.

God Purposes to Visit Us

God shows this tender mercy in that He purposes to visit us: "Through the tender mercy of our God; whereby the dayspring from on high *hath visited us*."

Notice that God has not merely pitied us from a distance, but

He has Himself *visited us*. Such an expression is full of holy thought. A *visit* from God, what must it be! "What is man, that thou art mindful of him? and the son of man, that thou visitest him?" (Ps. 8:4). That He should stoop to leave His high abode and the majesty wherein He reigns to visit insignificant beings like ourselves? The Bible is a letter from Him, and we prize it beyond the finest gold, but an actual visit from God Himself, what shall we say of such a favor?

In what ways has the Lord shown His tender mercy in purposing to visit us? I answer, first, God's great visit to us was in *the incarnation of our blessed Lord and Savior Jesus Christ*. Scripture records many visits of God to men, but the most wonderful visit of all was when He came to live here for some thirty years or more and worked out our salvation. What but "tender mercy," hearty mercy, intense mercy, could bring the great God to visit so closely that He actually assumed our nature? Kings visit their subjects, but they do not take on their poverty, sickness, or sorrow. But our Lord came into our flesh. He veiled His Godhead in a robe of our inferior clay. O children, the Lord so visited you as to become a babe, and then a child, who lived with His parents in obedience and grew in stature as you must do. O working men, the Lord so visited you as to become a carpenter's son and to know all about your toil and weariness. O sons of men, Jesus Christ has visited you so as to be tempted in all points like as you are, though without sin (Heb. 4:15). He took our sickness and bore our infirmities. This was a kind of visit such as none could have thought of granting save the infinitely tender and merciful God. The Man is our next kinsman, a brother born for adversity. In all our affliction, He is afflicted. He is tenderness itself.

Remember that He not only took our nature but also dwelt among us in this world of sin and sorrow. The little planet of ours was made to burn with a superior light while the Creator sojourned here in human form. He trod the acres of Samaria and walked the hills of Judea. "Who went about doing good, and healing all that were oppressed of the devil" (Acts 10:38). He mingled among men with hardly any reservation. Being through His purity separate from sinners as to His character, yet He was the visitor of all men. He was found eating bread with a Pharisee, which perhaps is a more wonderful thing than when He ate with sinners. A fallen woman was not too far gone for Him to sit and talk with at the well, nor were any of the poor and ignorant too low for Him to care for them. He was bone of our bone and flesh of our flesh. His visit to us was therefore of the most intimate kind. He disdained no man's lowliness. He turned aside from no man's sin.

But remember that His visit was not merely to teach us and set us a divine example, but He so visited us that He went down into our condemnation that He might deliver us from it. He was made a curse for us, as it is written, "Cursed is every one that hangeth on a tree" (Gal. 3:13). He took our debts upon Him that He might pay them, minting His own heart to create the coinage. He gave His own self for us to bear all the woes that had fallen upon human nature through its departure from the ways of God. "Surely he hath borne our griefs, and carried our sorrows . . . and the LORD hath laid on him the iniquity of us all" (Isa. 53:4, 6). Our Lord so visited us as to become our ransom. This was a wonderful piece of tender mercy indeed. It excels all conception and speech. If for the first time you had heard of the visit of the Incarnate God to this world, you would be struck with a wonder that would last throughout all eternity, that God Himself should really condescend to such a deed as this. This is the heart of the gospel. To simply hear the bare statement of the fact is enough to make one leap for joy. Since God has visited not in the form of vengeance or as a cherub with a flaming sword but in the gentle person of that lowliest of the lowly who said, "Suffer the little children to come unto me" (Mark 10:14), we are made to see the tender mercy of our God. Nothing could be more tender than the divine appearance of the Man of Sorrows.

To this day we are visited by God in other respects, but with equal mercy. *The proclamation of the gospel* in a nation or to an individual is a visit of God's mercy. Whenever you hear the gospel, whether you receive it or not, know that the kingdom of God has come near to you. God visits you in tender mercy in that by the gospel He tells you that there is a way of salvation. It is a monstrosity of iniquity that men who have sinned should refuse to accept God's pardoning love. How can anyone so hate his own soul? Surely the devils would not have believed that there could exist a race of creatures so hardened as to refuse the love that visits them in grace. Men sin not only against God but also against their own interests when they turn aside from the call of disinterested goodness and refuse salvation through Him who loved us even to the death. That which God has so tenderly and heartily worked out in the gift of His dear Son to die for us ought to be received with eagerness.

God has also visited some of us in a more remarkable manner still, for *by the Holy Spirit He has entered into our hearts* and changed our lives. He has turned our affections toward that which is right by enlightening our judgments. He has led us to the confession of sin and brought us to the acceptance of His mercy through the atoning blood. What a visit this is! This visit of the Holy Ghost, when He comes to dwell in us, is surpassingly condescending. I have often said that I never know which to admire most, the incarnation of the Son of God or the indwelling of the Spirit of God. The Holy Spirit does not take a pure body for His own, but He makes our bodies to be His temples. He dwells not in one but in tens of thousands. He dwells in us notwithstanding all our provocations and rebellions. Oh, this is tender mercy! Who can describe it? Sweet Spirit, gentle Spirit, how can You abide with me? O heavenly Dove, how can You find rest in such a soul as mine? Yet without You we are undone, and therefore we adore the tender mercy that makes You bear with us so long and work in us so graciously till You have conformed us to the image of the Firstborn. We are melted by the love of the Spirit—the communion of the Holy Spirit by which the Lord has visited us.

Often, since our first visitation by the Lord, I trust *we have had special visits from Him*, bringing with them rapturous joys, singular deliverances, and countless blessings. "The love of God is shed abroad in our hearts by the Holy Ghost which is given unto us" (Rom. 5:5). The Lord has visited us in the night and drawn close to our spirit, and so He has preserved us. We have enjoyed near and dear communion with the Father and His Son. When we were depressed in spirit, burdened with unusual cares, or weeping over heartbreaking situations, the mercy of our God has made the dayspring from on high to visit us at just such times.

Our life is bright with these visits as the sky with stars. The visits of God to His own children are proofs of the heartiness, the intensity, the tenderness of His mercy.

God Visits Us As the Dayspring from on High

"Whereby the dayspring from on high hath visited us." This means the dawning in the east, the rising of the sun at break of day. God does not come to us in Christ or by His Spirit as a tempest, as when He came to Paran with ten thousand of His holy ones in all the pomp of His fiery law (Deut. 33:2). But He has visited us as a smiling morning, which in gentle glory floods the world with joy.

While this gospel visitation is apparently less in splendor than that of the law, yet it is not deficient in true glory. God has not visited us as a candle that only was sufficient to light our darkness but could not change it into day. The Lord has visited us with the dawn of day.

Moreover, the Lord has come not as a blaze that will soon die down but as a light that will last forever. After the long, dark, and cold night of our misery, the Lord comes in the fittest and most effectual manner. Neither lightning nor candle nor flaming meteor would do, but the Lord comes as the sun that begins the day.

The Lord's visitation to us is as the dayspring because *it suits our eye*. As the eye is suited to light, and light to the eye, it is so in the realm of grace. Daybreak in the east has not the blaze of burning noon about it, but it peeps forth as a gray light that gradually increases to the perfect day. So did the Lord Jesus come dimly at first to Bethlehem, but He will appear in all the glory of the Father. So does the Spirit of God come to us in gradual progress. There is a sweet suitableness in the grace of God to the heart and in the renewed heart to the grace of God. The revelation of God to each person is made in a form and manner tenderly agreeable to the condition and capacity of the person. I sometimes think the gospel was made exactly to meet my case. Do you not think the same of it? The morning light suits your eye as exactly as if there were no other creature to behold it. And so in divine tenderness the Lord has made His visits suitable to our sorrow and even to our weakness. He shows us just enough of Himself to delight us without utterly overwhelming us with the excess of brightness. He might have come in the majesty of His grace to us at the first, but then we were not able to bear it. He gave us milk when we were babes in grace but meat when were ready to eat with Him. All the visits of God to us are merciful, but in those of the dawn of grace we see tenderness as well as mercy.

The visits of God are like the dayspring because *they end our darkness*. The dayspring vanishes the night. Without noise or effort, it removes the ebony blackness and sows the earth with orient pearl. Night stretches her bat's wing and flies before the arrows of the advancing sun. So the coming of Jesus into our hearts takes away the darkness of ignorance, sorrow, carelessness, fear, and despair. Our night is ended once for all when we behold God visiting us in Christ Jesus. Our day may cloud over, but night will not return. If Jesus is seen by faith, you will need no candles of human confidence or sparks of feelings and impressions. The beholding of Christ shall be the ending of all night for you. "They looked unto him, and were lightened: and their faces were not ashamed" (Ps. 34:5).

I like to think of Christ as coming into the world as the morning light because He comes *with such a largeness of present blessing*—blessing immeasurable, unlimited. Some people are always for measuring out how much Christ can or will do. They would allot so many beams of light to so many eyes and limit the light by the number of those who rejoice in it. But Jesus is the light of the world. He comes from on high to shed light over the whole universe, even as the sun goes forth from one end of heaven to the other and nothing is hid from its heat. Jesus appears as the light that lights every man that comes into the world (John 1:9). Whoever is willing to receive that light is free to do so (John 1:7). This light comes even to those who hate it, thus leaving them without excuse: "the light shineth in darkness; and the darkness comprehended it not" (John 1:5) and "this is the condemnation, that light is come into the world, and men loved darkness rather than light, because their deeds were evil" (John 3:19). When the Lord comes to men, His blessings are infinite. You might as well try measuring the length and breadth of the sunlight with a yardstick as try to measure the tender mercy of our God in the revelation of our Lord Jesus Christ.

When the Lord visits us, it is as the dayspring because *He brings us hope of a greater glory yet to come.* The first coming of Christ did not manifest everything. The dayspring is not the noon, but it is a sure guarantee of it. And so is the first advent the pledge of the glory to be revealed. The sun never rises in error to suddenly set again but rises to complete its course. When we receive a visit from the Lord, it may be in the way of rebuke or of feeble hope, but let us be patient, for the dawn shall grow with constant increase of light. There is no fear of its dying down into the old sinful darkness. An eternal noon is the destiny of all whose eyes have beheld the Christ.

This coming of the Lord and of His light so gradually and yet so lavishly, so fittingly and yet so effectually, does it not fill you with gratitude? Every little bird rejoices in the rising of the sun. God has made the sun to rise so graciously that not even a sparrow trembles at it but chirps with confidence its happy praises. God has made the sun to rise that every tiny cup of every flower that blooms opens to drink in the golden light and is refreshed by it. The coming of Christ is just such to us, even to the least and feeblest of us. It is not a stupendous blessing that crushes us by its enormous weight or a mysterious revelation that confounds us by its profundity, but it is simplicity itself, gentleness itself. Nonetheless, the coming of Christ is all the more grand and sublime because it is so simple and tender. Let us bless God that He visits us and that when He visits us, it is as the dayspring from on high.

God Visits Us in Our Very Lowest Estate

"To give knowledge of salvation unto his people by the remission of their sins." It appears that *God comes to visit us when we are in our sins.* If the plan of salvation were that we had to get out of our sins and then God would come to us, it might be full of mercy, but it would not be tender mercy. Let it never be forgotten that "God commendeth his love toward us, in that, while we were yet sinners, Christ died for us" (Rom. 5:8). The visits of God spring from grace, pure grace, altogether unmixed with any merit or claim on our part. God comes to us as the morning that waits for no man. When we had no good about us whatsoever, God's tender mercy visited us, even as the sun rises upon the just and upon the unjust. God will not mar the magnificence of His goodness by asking our pitiful penny of merit as a payment for it, but He gives freely in accordance to the riches of His grace. As He makes His rain to water the fields of the miser as well as those of the kind, so He gives His bounty to the worst of men. Let us learn this and imitate this, for thus we shall know the tender mercy of God. To copy the divine example will be the surest method of coming to an understanding of it.

Furthermore, *our God visits us when we are in darkness*. When we are in such darkness as to know nothing, see nothing, believe nothing, hope nothing, even then the Lord's mercy comes to us. Is not this tenderness? God does not send grace to us because we already have something that may be viewed as prevenient and preparatory, but the prevenient and the preparatory are of His grace, and He comes in love to bring these with Him, to those who as yet know nothing of His light and life. They are in the dark, and He creates their day.

Did you notice that it is said "to them that *sit* in darkness?" This is more than being in the dark. The man who *sits* in darkness does so because he feels that his case is hopeless. A lost traveller in the darkest night has lost his road and finally crouches in a rocky shelter in despair of finding the track. It is part of the tender mercy of God that He visits those who despond and are motionless in dread inactivity. Those who have lost hope are lost indeed, and such the Savior comes to save.

Then it is added, *"and in the shadow of death."* Did you ever feel that shadow? It has a horrible influence. Chill and cold, it freezes the marrow of the bones and stops the lifeflow in the veins. Death stands over the man, and if his hand does not smite, yet his shadow darkens joy and chills hope, numbing the heart and making life itself a mode of death. The shadow of death is a confusion of mind, depression of spirit, dread of the unknown, horror at the past, and terror of the future. But the Lord has come forth to deliver the captive and save those appointed unto death. Knowing your guilt, the Lord bids you look up: "Behold the Lamb of God, which taketh away the sin of the world" (John 1:29). Look and live; look and be delivered at once, even from the horrible death shadow that broods over you. You seem to be forgotten of God, left out of the registry of hope, but yet to you has Jesus come "to give light." Is this not *tender* mercy? If He had not come to shine on such as us, I would never have been saved. Jesus does everything for us from the beginning. He is the Alpha even as He must be the Omega. He comes to us in darkness and under the grim shadow of death, and there and then reveals His love to us.

God's Visits Have Wonderful Results

"To give light to them that sit in darkness and in the shadow of death, to guide them into the way of peace." Imagine a caravan in the desert that has lost its way and is famishing. The sun has long gone down, and the darkness has caused everyone's heart to droop. All around them is a waste of sand and utter darkness. There they must remain and die unless they can find the track. Hungry and thirsty, they are so fearful they cannot sleep. Heavier and heavier the night comes down, and the damp chill in their tents has frozen their souls. What is to be done? How they watch! But no star comes to comfort them. At last the watchman cries, "The morning comes!" It breaks over the sea of sand and, what is better, reveals a way-mark that points the way to their track. The dayspring has saved them from swift destruction by discovering the way of peace.

When the Lord Jesus Christ visits us, He actually brings light to our darkness, really leads into the way, and makes that way a way of peace to us. Put it all together and remember what the Lord has done. You did not know the way once, nor would you have found it apart from His Spirit visiting you as the dayspring.

Even when you saw the way, you were still powerless to reach it of yourself. Jesus came near and actually guided your feet into that way. He put your feet upon a rock and established your goings. It was the Lord shining upon your road that made it a way of perfect peace. Peace in our text means prosperity, plenty, rest, and joy. Since the Lord has visited you, have you not gone forth with joy and been led forth with peace (Isa. 55:12)?

If the tender mercy of God has visited us and done so much more for us than I can tell, let us exhibit tender mercy in our dealings with others. It is a wretched business for a man to call himself a Christian and have a soul that never peeps out from between his own ribs. It is horrible to be living to get to heaven and yet never to live to bless others and ease the misery of a moaning world. It is all nonsense to regard religion as a selfish spiritual trade by which we save our own souls. Unless your faith tears you away from yourself and makes you live for something nobler than even your own spiritual good, you have not passed out of the darkness into the light of God. Only the way of unselfishness is the way of peace. I ask you to think tenderly of all poor people. These are hard times. Let those who have more than they actually need always be ready to relieve distress in others.

Yet *"where sin abounded, grace did much more abound." Oh, for an angel's tongue to tell of the wondrous mystery! My poor pen is quite unequal to the tremendous task. How does one attempt to describe the grace that so gloriously abounded in our Lord upon the cross? The grace that flashed so favorably from those languid eyes; the grace that fell in cleansing drops from those opened veins; the grace that poured in torrents from that pierced side; the grace that heaved and tossed and struggled convulsively in those tortured limbs; the grace that fought and wrestled and at last conquered in that anguished spirit; the grace that even then began interceding for the transgressors as Jesus prayed, "Father, forgive them; for they know not what they do" (Luke 23:34); the grace that cried with a mighty voice, "It is finished" (John 19:30), before the Savior bowed His head and gave up His spirit; the grace that ascended out up on high, leading captivity captive and giving gifts unto men (Eph. 4:8). Of this grace I dare not write upon further. May it be your happy lot to sail upon that sea of grace, for fathom it you never can! May you drink from that fountain of grace, for you shall never be able to drink it dry! May God give you the bliss of knowing in your own experience how much grace abounds through the atoning sacrifice of Christ upon the cross!*

Chapter Four

Grace Abounding

But where sin abounded, grace did much more abound—Romans 5:20.

THERE HAS BEEN A LONG BATTLE in this world between man's sin and God's grace. If it had been a fight between man's sin and God's justice, it would have soon come to an end. Imagine the flames of hell and observe what God's justice can do when it comes into conflict with human guilt. When God goes to war against ungodliness, His might is indeed terrible. Divine justice makes short work of sin. It treads it under foot and stamps it out, for God hates sin with a perfect hatred. When God's anger is aroused against sin, He tears it in pieces as the lion tears his prey in his fury. Fortunately, the conflict is not between justice and sin but between grace and sin. God's milder attribute of mercy has entered the field, and in our text Paul tells us the result of the battle. It looked for a time as if sin would gain the victory, for it abounded more and more. But at the last the banner of grace waved triumphantly over the battlefield, for "where sin abounded, grace did much more abound."

Federal Headship

The Apostle Paul has been writing about the principle of representation, the federal headship, first of Adam and then of our Lord Jesus Christ. He has described our fall and ruin under our first federal head and our salvation and redemption by our second covenant Head. It seems at first sight as if setting up Adam as the representative man had been the means of making sin to abound, because as soon as sin overcame Adam, it overcame the whole race of mankind. It appears it would have been better to have put every man on probation on his own account and to let him stand or fall according to his behavior. Sin seems to have won a comparatively easy victory by overthrowing the whole race with a single blow.

Certainly, sin did gain a great victory in the garden of Eden, and it abounded. But Paul shows that it was by this very principle of representation that "grace did much more abound," for it is through the death of One, even Jesus Christ, that all believers live. It is by the righteousness of this One that a multitude whom no man can number shall attain everlasting life. It appears to me that if the other system had been adopted, where each one stands or falls by himself, there would have been no hope of salvation for any one of the whole race of mankind. We believe that the angels stood or fell according to their own account. Satan was not the federal head of the angels, and consequently, the others fell only by choosing to join his treason and without hope of their restoration to God's favor: "the angels which kept not their first estate, but left their own habitation, he hath reserved in everlasting chains under darkness unto the judgment of the great day" (Jude 6).

I think it highly probable that had you and I been left to stand or fall on our own account, we would have fallen to rise no more. But now, as we fell in the person of one representative, it has become possible for us to rise through another Representative. As many as have believed in Jesus have risen from the fall of Adam and are delivered from the death that was the consequence of Adam's sin, being made alive in Christ Jesus by a new spiritual life in virtue of union with the risen Lord. By the federal headship of Adam, sin did abound, and torrents of iniquity inundated the whole human race. But by the federal headship of Christ, grace does much more abound so that all who believe in Him shall be eternally saved.

The Law Increases the Weight of Sin

The first part of the verse illustrated another truth: "the law entered, that the offense might abound." Through no fault of its own, but through our depravity, the law increases the weight of sin.

We know that if we do not give our child commands, he cannot disobey us. But the moment a command is given, the natural inclination of the child is to disobey and turn the command into an occasion for sin. The more commands God gives, the more possibilities for man to sin. The fault is not in the command but in the response of man's wicked heart that rebels against the command. Paul says, "I had not known sin, but by the law" (Rom. 7:7). He would have been just as truly a sinner in himself, but the sinfulness would not have come out if it had not been for the law's prohibitions and restrictions against which he rebelled. The law exposes the sin in a person's life by conviction and allows the person to see it in its true character. The law comes like a policeman with a search warrant and says, "There is a criminal concealed here, and I have come to uncover him." Despite the protests against it, the law will search until even those who do not suspect sin will see the true nature of their heart.

It seems a very dreadful thing that the effect of the law should be to make the sinner worse than he was before: "the law entered, that the offense might abound." But that is just where our text comes in: "where sin abounded, grace did much more abound." The more needful the law's exposure of, the more glorious the grace that cleanses from the sin. The law like a candle shows me my blackness. But that same revelation also shows me the precious blood of Jesus that makes me whiter than snow. As I hear the thunders of Sinai and am full of terror as the lightning sets the sky ablaze, I turn to the dear, patient Lamb of God and see Him suffering for me. I say to Him, "Oh, what wondrous grace it must have been by which You delivered me from all this terrible wrath. Blessed Lamb of God, how much I owe You, for You have hushed the law's loud thunder and given my soul a quiet and safe hiding place." The work of the law upon the enlightened soul is like a sharp needle that goes through the soul, but it draws the golden thread of mercy with it. It is like the sharp plow that breaks up the ground and prepares the soil for the seed that in due time shall bring forth the harvest to God's praise and glory. Whenever the entrance of the law makes the offense to abound, may God grant us grace to receive the gospel so that grace shall much more abound!

The Place Called Calvary

The place called Calvary is the spot where sin did most abound, yet where grace abounded even more. Look in at the council chamber of the Sanhedrin and hear them charge the Son of God with blasphemy. See Him hurried away to Pilate's hall and to Herod's judgment seat, "despised and rejected of men" (Isa. 53:3), and behold how they mocked Him, how they plucked out His hair, defiled His blessed face with their accursed spit, crowned Him with thorns, and assailed Him with insult upon insult and cruelty upon cruelty, and then say if sin did not indeed abound there. See Him toiling painfully through the crowded streets, scoffed by the multitude but mourned by the daughters of Jerusalem. Watch Him as at last He ascends the hill of doom, see Him hanging on the cross in indescribable agony while the heartless spectators jeer and scoff and make a jest even of His dying cries, and then say if sin did not abound there. What foaming billows of iniquity rolled up around that accursed tree, swelling and rising until they completely immersed the Lord of life and glory in their horrible depths! Yes, truly sin abounded there. Surely it was the darkest day in human history. They killed the Son of God and cast Him out of the vineyard, saying, "This is the heir; come, let us kill him, and let us seize on his inheritance"

(Matt. 21:38). Sin abounded so much that it put out the light of the sun. Sin was so heavy it cracked the solid earth and rent the rocks asunder, causing the graves to open while the great veil of the temple was torn from top to bottom.

Yet "where sin abounded, grace did much more abound." Oh, for an angel's tongue to tell of the wondrous mystery! My poor pen is quite unequal to the tremendous task. How does one attempt to describe the grace that so gloriously abounded in our Lord upon the cross? The grace that flashed so favorably from those languid eyes; the grace that fell in cleansing drops from those opened veins; the grace that poured in torrents from that pierced side; the grace that heaved and tossed and struggled convulsively in those tortured limbs; the grace that fought and wrestled and at last conquered in that anguished spirit; the grace that even then began interceding for the transgressors as Jesus prayed, "Father, forgive them; for they know not what they do' (Luke 23:34); the grace that cried with a mighty voice, "It is finished" (John 19:30), before the Savior bowed His head and gave up His spirit; the grace that ascended out up on high, leading captivity captive and giving gifts unto men (Eph. 4:8). Of this grace I dare not write upon further. May it be your happy lot to sail upon that sea of grace, for fathom it you never can! May you drink from that fountain of grace, for you shall never be able to drink it dry! May God give you the bliss of knowing in your own experience how much grace abounds through the atoning sacrifice of Christ upon the cross!

Oh, that my soul were aglow as the soul of Whitefield used to be while I plead my Savior's cause! Nothing so clearly shows the terrible depravity of human nature as this, that man has become so utterly wicked and debased as to believe that Christ is not the Savior! What a vile wretch man must be, and what an evil thing human nature must be, when any can deliberately doubt the power of Christ to save the lost! The inspired declaration is that "he is able also to save them to the uttermost that come unto God by him, seeing he ever liveth to make intercession for them" (Heb. 7:25). Yet this wicked heart of ours finds it impossible to believe it until the Holy Spirit comes with supernatural energy and enlightens the understanding, sways the will, controls the judgment, and brings the soul to rest in Jesus Christ. How guilty must we be that we will not believe that what God says is true though millions of witnesses before the throne of heaven attest to the truth that "where sin abounded, grace did much more abound."

Man's Nature

Man's nature is a fourth illustration of where grace abounded. Look at Adam in the garden of Eden, a noble being supreme among all the creatures about him. All the birds and beasts come at his call and yield obedience to his command. But do you see the serpent coiled around the tree? That is the brute embodiment of sin, and it has come there to do incalculable damage. Wait a little while, and you may see Adam and Eve driven out of the garden where they were once so happy, for the sin to which they so readily yielded has brought a heavy curse upon them and all their descendants. As you read the stern sentences pronounced upon each of them by the lips of Jehovah Himself, you realize that in their case sin has indeed abounded. Then you recall the principle of representation and realize that Adam's fall involved the fall of every one of us.

If you want to see how sin has abounded, just take a look around your world and see the overwhelming evidence. I need not go into repulsive descriptions of how fallen creatures have come to live, but we must each confess that apart from the providence and grace of God we might have been as bad. If you want to see further what ruin sin has wrought, I would take you to the graveyard. How the noble being whom God made to have dominion over all the works of His hands has fallen! This is what sin has brought man down to—an empty skull and a few dry bones.

But I will not linger over that dark part of the subject. Think how grace has much more abounded even where sin did most abound. Grace comes in and finds man under sentence of death, hopeless, and polluted. What does grace do in such a case? I answer by pointing to that wondrous vision that John had in

Patmos when he saw "one like unto the Son of man. . . . His head and his hairs were white like wool, as white as snow; and his eyes were as a flame of fire; and his feet like unto fine brass, as if they burned in a furnace; and his voice as the sound of many waters. And he had in his right hand seven stars: and out of his mouth went a sharp twoedged sword: and his countenance was as the sun shineth in his strength" (Rev. 1:13–16). Who is this from whom all heaven rings with hallelujahs while hell trembles at His word and millions upon earth own allegiance to Him? Why, 'tis the man Christ Jesus, who once slept as a helpless babe in His mother's arms, who afterwards toiled at the carpenter's bench at Nazareth, and who breathed out His earthly life amid the untold agonies of Calvary. He is now exalted to His Father's right hand, "far above all principality, and power, and might, and dominion, and every name that is named, not only in this world, but also in that which is to come" (Eph. 1:21).

"That is fine," you say, "but we are not up there with Him." But faith says that we are if we are truly trusting in Jesus, for "God, who is rich in mercy, for his great love wherewith he loved us, even when we were dead in sins, hath quickened us together with Christ, (by grace ye are saved;) and hath raised us up together, and made us sit together in heavenly places in Christ Jesus: that in the ages to come he might shew the exceeding riches of his grace in his kindness toward us through Christ Jesus" (Eph. 2:4–7). Now you see how gloriously true our text is. Sin did us untold damage, but grace has given us more than sin ever took away. Sin robbed us of silver, but grace has given us gold. Sin threw us down among the masses of this fallen race, but grace has lifted us up and set us among the children of God by faith in Christ Jesus. "Beloved, now are we the sons of God, and it doth not yet appear what we shall be: but we know that, when he shall appear, we shall be like him; for we shall see him as he is" (1 John 3:2). That is how grace has abounded.

In Us

Many of us have known the depths of a life where sin abounded. But now a great change has come through grace, and we have been made new creatures in Christ Jesus. You know that it is very often the case that those who have been the greatest sinners become the greatest saints, and those who have been the devil's captains and generals become the boldest and bravest soldiers of the cross when converted. Indeed, many of us ought to love much because we have been forgiven much. Divine mercy has covered and blotted out a vast mass of sin that we had committed. Remembering with humility and shame all our past offenses, we pray that we may prove in all our future what holy and useful men and women God's grace can make of us. Surely you will not serve God worse than you served the devil. When you had a bad master, you were a good servant to him. But now that you have the best master you can ever have, do not be a poor servant to Him. May the Lord grant that great grace may abound in all who have been great sinners!

But not all of us were great sinners. Kindly turn to the little book that records your life history written out upon the pages of your memory. As you look over those pages, what do you think of yourself? If you find something to make you feel highly about yourself, you must not be thinking at all. But those who really do think must see much in their past lives that causes them to blush. Looking back upon the years since we first came to Christ, what a multitude of sins we have committed! If our own children had treated us as badly as we have treated our heavenly Father, what would we have done with them? What a marvel of patience our heavenly Father has been in His dealings with us! I look at my pastoral work, and I have to confess that sin has abounded there. I look at my private life, and I have to own that sin has abounded there. As you look at your life, I believe that you must say with sorrow that sin has abounded there. But has not grace also abounded? Ay, that it has, for "where sin abounded, grace did much more abound." Do not ever get into such a state of heart as to groan over yourself so that you cannot praise the Lord for His abounding grace. Oh, do praise Him and bless Him, for He well deserves to be praised! Sin abounds, so be humble; but grace much more abounds, therefore be thankful. Sin abounds, so be watchful; but grace does much more abound, therefore be confident that God will give you the victory through Him that loves you.

In This World

Stand upon your watchtower and look over the world as far as you can. A great proportion of it is still shrouded in the dense darkness of heathenism. Uncounted millions bow before blocks of wood and stone. Think of the vast multitudes who put their trust in Allah and his false prophet Mohammed. Then remember with sorrow how large a proportion of those who are called Christians are simply worshippers of Mary instead of believers in Jesus, or who bow before images, icons, relics, crosses, and I know not what. If we turn to Protestant Christianity, what a vast mass of hypocrisy, formality, inconsistency, and everything else that is evil is mixed with that which is genuine and true! All over the world sin abounds. See how many lands are still cursed by war. What infamies are perpetrated in all our great cities! God must have been amazingly patient to have borne so long with our wicked race. As the flood of Noah's days was universal, so sin covers the earth today, prevailing over the tops of the mountains and abounding in all the valleys and plains.

How depressing if we did not believe that grace shall abound over sin. But the day is coming when suddenly the pedestal upon which any false god is seated shall be shaken and fall and when the crescent of Mohammed shall wane forever. All that is false about religion shall be judged, and the devil and all his hosts shall be cast into the lake of fire and brimstone to be tormented day and night forever and ever. The day is coming when the people on every island and every continent shall hear the joyful sound of the gospel of God's grace. From Ethiopia to India to China to Japan, we shall no longer hear the praises of any false god, but we shall delight as the confession rings that Jesus Christ, the Son of David, is also the Son of God, King of kings and Lord of lords, and their own and only Savior. The little spring that burst up like a rippling rivulet from the foot of Calvary's cross has swollen into a mighty river even now. The tides of the gospel are swelling and growing, and the day is coming when, like a mighty ocean, the gospel shall cover the whole earth as the waters cover the deep, and floating across that sea of glory shall be heard the millennial anthem: "The kingdoms of this world are become the kingdoms of our Lord, and of his Christ, and he shall reign for ever and ever" (Rev. 11:15). Hallelujah! Hallelujah! Hallelujah!

Then, at the last, we who have believed in Jesus shall be gathered with Him in that great city, the new Jerusalem, whose twelve gates are twelve pearls, whose walls are jasper, and whose street is of "pure gold, like unto clear glass" (Rev. 21:18). This is the city of which John says, "I saw no temple therein: for the Lord God Almighty and the Lamb are the temple of it. And the city had no need of the sun, neither of the moon, to shine in it: for the glory of God did lighten it, and the Lamb is the light thereof" (Rev. 21:22–23). What a day that shall be, and we shall get there in due time. Then, when looking down from our serene abode, we shall be able to read the whole drama of human history, from the creation to the fall of Adam, from the fall to the cross of Christ, and then to the final consummation of all things. There we will discover the summation of all that occurred as this: "Where sin abounded, grace did much more abound."

If it should be my happy privilege up there upon some sunny mount to preach upon this theme in more flaming words than I can today, all of you who are of a kindred spirit with me will help to tell the story to the principalities and powers in heavenly places. And the harpers standing on the sea of glass will strike their harps afresh and sing again the song of Moses the servant of God and the song of the Lamb, and their songs will be in harmony with our theme: "Where sin abounded, grace did much more abound." So let us go forth to our various occupations believing that though sin abounds, grace shall yet more abound. Let us live so that all may see how grace abounds in us. And let us help to spread the wondrous story of what grace has done for us, that others may seek that grace for themselves.

What grace will God give? He will give all manner of grace. There is grace not only in fullness but in all variety treasured up in Christ Jesus. As our needs are many, so the forms in which grace blesses us are many. Do you feel like a little child studying God's ABC book in God's great school and ignorant of the deep things of God? Then if you want to understand with all the saints what are the heights and breadths and to know the love of Christ that passes knowledge, He will give you grace. He will give grace to instruct. He will make you to know even as you are known (1 Cor. 13:12). He shall give you His Holy Spirit, who shall lead you into all truth and take the things of Christ and show them to you (John 16:13). He will give instructing grace.

Chapter Five

Grace and Glory

The LORD will give grace and glory—Psalm 84:11.

IT IS VERY WISE to look within ourselves to discover our weakness and spiritual poverty, but it is very unwise to be always dwelling upon that weakness and poverty, forgetting that our strength does not lie there nor are our riches to be found in ourselves. Let us look within to be humbled but not to be made unbelieving. Look within to be driven from all confidence in ourselves but never so as to shake our absolute confidence in God. Our verse from the psalm calls us away from seeking the living among the dead and from searching for precious jewels among the dross and refuse. It directs us to the living God Himself, the overflowing fountain of every good thing, to our Father, whose arm is not shortened that it cannot save and whose ear is not heavy that He cannot hear. Jehovah Himself, the infinite, eternal, everlasting, inimitable *I AM*, will give grace and glory. Though you may think that you have no grace, He will give it to you. Though you may fear that you shall never obtain glory, yet He can and will bestow it upon you. "The LORD will give grace and glory." He takes us away from leaning on the broken reeds of our self-reliance and calls us away to the rock of our salvation, where we may rest with security.

"He will *give* grace and glory." "Give" takes us off from our natural legality of self-trust. I think we are all apt to go back to the bondage of Mount Sinai. We are like those foolish Galatians who were "bewitched" so that we do "not obey the truth," but "having begun in the Spirit," we seek to be "made perfect by the flesh" (Gal. 3:1, 3). Having been saved already by faith, we so often try to be perfected by the works of the law.

It is strange that after having felt the whip of legal bondage, we should wish to go back to the brick-kilns of Egypt and to be once more slaves. The text says He "will *give* grace and glory," which are the very opposite of wage and put us on the footing of grace. What a blessed thing to see a finger from the sky that beckons us away from underneath the quaking mountain where even Moses confessed that he did altogether fear and quake (Heb. 12:21). It is a blessed thing to be set free from the thunderings and lightnings and the voice as of a trumpet, and to be brought to the blood that speaks better things than that of Abel (Heb. 12:24), and to hear God speaking concerning His great and unspeakable gifts to us!

There are two great and splendid gifts that God here declares He will bestow: first, the gift of grace, and then, the gift of glory.

God Will Give Grace

To whom will He give grace? Broadly understood, we may say that *He will give grace to His own chosen ones.* So is it in the covenant of grace. "I will have mercy on whom I will have mercy, and I will have compassion on whom I will have compassion. So then it is not of him that willeth, nor of him that runneth, but of God that sheweth mercy" (Rom. 9:15–16). Grace is a most sovereign thing. God has the right to give it where He pleases, and He takes care that the sovereignty shall be seen. Some have gone far into sin, perhaps to the very verge of destruction and last hour of life, but He will give them grace. There is not one upon whom His electing love has set the broad arrow of the kingdom who shall pass away without receiving grace.

God will give grace to all those who are specially redeemed by Christ. As many as Christ has redeemed and purchased by His blood shall be His, for we hear Him say, "The good shepherd giveth his life for the sheep" (John 10:11). Christ loved His church and gave Himself for it. The chosen are spoken of in this manner: "These were redeemed from among men" (Rev. 14:4). And although the redemption of Christ has its universal aspect very plainly taught in God's Word, yet there is a special redemption besides: "we trust in the living God, who is the Saviour of all men, specially of those that believe" (1 Tim. 4:10). That special redemption is of such a kind that all those who are concerned in it He will give grace. Not one member of that body that Christ has redeemed shall be maimed or destroyed. Christ will give each of these His grace.

Thus, we have great confidence as we declare the gospel that God will give grace to those who believe. We cannot tell, except by marks and evidences, who those specially redeemed ones are, but it may be said that the Lord will give grace *to every believing soul.* If you put your whole reliance upon the atonement of Christ, He will give you grace. Though your faith should be so slender that it seems to be nothing but a bruised reed, He will not break your faith but will give you grace. Though our spiritual life may seem to be so dim as to be nothing but as smoking flax, He will not quench it but will give grace. If you rest in Christ, though there may be much fear and mistrust mingled with your reliance, yet He will give grace. "For whosoever shall call upon the name of the Lord shall be saved" (Rom. 10:13). It does not say how loud he is to call, but if his call be ever so faint, yet if he does but call he shall have grace. "Him that cometh unto me I will in no wise cast out" (John 6:37). It does not say whether he comes walking or running or crawling, but if he does but come he shall not be cast out. If you believe in the Lord Jesus Christ, then of you it may be said, "The LORD will give grace."

The same may be said *to every repenting sinner.* If you abhor your sin, if you resolve by God's strength to give it up, if the sweetness of sin has turned to bitterness, if it is like gravel between your teeth, then He will give you grace. When you are thoroughly sick of sin and self, He will give you grace to joy and rejoice in Christ.

The same shall be said of *all those who are prayerful*. He will give grace to all who seek it with earnest hearts through the Savior. At the mercy seat, whether you are a saint or a sinner, if you draw near to God in sincere prayer, He has given you some grace already, and He will give you more. Every time that you go to God with a true-hearted confidence in prayer, put this before you emblazoned in letters of gold, "He will give grace."

I might continue these instances as to different characteristics, but rest assured that if you are a believer and you use prayer and repentance, you shall find His promise true *in all your conditions.* If you go forth to work for God, He will give grace. You shall not go to warfare at your own expense. In the vineyard you shall find Him furnishing you with tools and strength equal to the day. He will give grace. And if you are laid aside from active service and made to lie upon that bed that grows harder every hour until the bed becomes a misery, still He will give grace. Perhaps you are untried at suffering, but He will give you grace. Perhaps you are naturally of an impatient spirit, then wait upon Him. He knows how to bring your spirit down one way and lift it up another. He will give grace.

But to turn the subject a moment, let us ask, *What grace will God give?* He will give all manner of grace. There is grace not only in fullness but in all variety treasured up in Christ Jesus. As our needs are many, so the forms in which grace blesses us are many. Do you feel like a little child studying God's ABC book in God's great school and ignorant of the deep things of God? Then if you want to understand with all the saints what are the heights and breadths and to know the love of Christ that passes knowledge, He will give you grace. He will give *grace to instruct.* He will make you to know even as you are known (1 Cor. 13:12). He shall give you His Holy Spirit, who shall lead you into all truth and take the things of Christ and show them to you (John 16:13). He will give instructing grace.

Perhaps you are surrounded with difficulties. There are mountains behind and the rolling sea in front, and you ask, "What shall I do?" "Fear ye not, stand still, and see the salvation of the LORD" (Exod. 14:13). He will give you *delivering grace.* If He does not give money to meet your needs, He will give you grace to bear your poverty. If He does not give you the health to rise from your sickbed, He will give you grace to bear it and even to rejoice in the Lord always. He will give grace. If you will only wait, you have *directing grace.* You shall hear a voice near you saying, "This is the way, walk ye in it" (Isa. 30:21). Do as David did when he said, "Bring hither the ephod" (1 Sam. 23:9), that he might ask of God's priests what he should do. If you will wait until Christ, God's great High Priest, takes the sacred Urim and Thummim, He shall be pleased to send light into your soul and directing grace to guide you on your way. "He that trusteth in the LORD, mercy shall compass him about" (Ps. 32:10).

Perhaps your need is not so much instruction and direction as it is comfort. Perhaps you are feeling depressed and sunk in spirit. God can give you grace. An eighth of an ounce of grace is often better than a pound of whatever the world might offer. What a blessed revival of spirit God can give to His downcast ones!

I think it is one of the delights of the Spirit of God to comfort mourners. I know it is, because Jesus spoke the name of the Comforter because we need most His comfort to strengthen and fortify us for all life's endurances. We need most the comfort of the Holy Spirit, and that is His gracious occupation. He delights to comfort all who are tired and mourn.

When a man has many titles, he will naturally choose to be best known by the one that he likes best, and the Holy Spirit uses this name of the Comforter, though He has many more names besides. When you are troubled and distracted, tossed with tempest and not comforted, Jesus comes and says, "He will give you grace." If He gives you grace, you need not wish to have your trouble removed, but like Paul be satisfied with the gracious promise: "My grace is sufficient for thee" (2 Cor. 12:9).

Possibly you are not troubled now. Beware of that. Be thankful and pray that you may not be. "Lead us not into temptation, but deliver us from evil" (Matt. 6:13). But it is possible that you now need grace to lead you to make advances in *inward sanctification,* and though this may seem very difficult to you in the position in which you are placed and burdened as you are with inward corruptions, yet He will give grace. You have a bad temper. Down with it! "I cannot," you say. But He will give grace. You have a proud spirit. Away with it! "I cannot conquer it," you cry. He will give grace. Your heart has grown lukewarm, and you must be revived. You say, "How?" He will give grace. Grace is the one thing that is needed to put the Christian into a healthy state of soul, and the promise of the Lord is exactly to this point. He will give grace. You must never say you cannot be holy. Never tell me you cannot grow to be as patient as Job or as believing as Abraham. Job received his patience and Abraham received his believing from God. God is not limited in His gifts to us. He is as ready to enrich us as He was to enrich those ancient ones. Go to Him with childlike confidence and say, "He will give grace."

You may need strength or protection or correction and rebuke. But whatever your great need, His grace will meet it. Come as poor Hannah and, though your lips move in silent prayer because of some very painful affliction, tell the Lord what it is. Whatever the wound may be, there is medicine that will bring the grace of healing. Wrap yourself in the promise that "He will give grace," and no problem is too big. There may be no change in your circumstances, but if He will give you grace, they will seem very different from what they were.

Perhaps you are shivering at the thought of the greatest enemy of all, namely, death. As you are getting old, perhaps you fear death's approach. Well, God will give grace, and though you must die, yet grace will enable you to go through the Jordan singing in its utmost depths, triumphing in the grace that will surely bring you safe to the other side. He will give grace to those who sincerely seek it.

But now, taking the same thought but putting it in another light, *in what manner will God give grace?*

He will give it sufficiently. He will give you as much grace as you need, though certainly none to spare. There was always enough manna for each day, but no more. There shall be abundant grace for abundant temptation or trial. And for those who are in many trials, there shall be grace yet superabundant.

He will give His grace *seasonably.* It shall always come when we need it. When the test or trial comes, your grace shall come. When you come to the point where you feel you must put your burden down, there shall be grace given that will strengthen your back to bear the load. You shall not meet with abounding grace when you do not require it, but just as your days so shall your strength be (Deut. 33:25).

God will also send His grace *readily*. You shall not have to tug and strain for it. You shall not have to labor and toil to win it. It shall drop upon you as the honey falling from the comb. It shall come as freely to you as the water bubbles up from the great spring. He will be a very present help in trouble and is as delighted to deliver you as you are to be delivered (Ps. 46:1).

And the grace shall come to you *constantly*—not occasionally or sometimes, but at all times, night and day. God shall never cease to bless you, for His mercy endures forever. If the earth should forget the covenant that God made for it with the sun and moon, if seedtimes and harvest should pass away as they must in the end times, yet though the mountains may depart and the hills be removed, still the covenant of His grace shall not depart from you. Grace shall come to you constantly.

Keep in mind one thing. Grace will come through the mediation of Christ. You shall get your grace from Him in whom it has pleased the Father that all fullness of deity may dwell (Col. 1:19). And in another sense, you shall get it mediately through the use of means. "I will yet for this be enquired of by the house of Israel, to do it for them" (Ezek. 36:37). He will give grace, but you must pray for it. He will give grace, but you must search the Scriptures to find it. He will give grace, but you must observe the means He has given. You must get in communion with God and draw near to Him. You must have your times of quiet retirement and still meditation, for although the Lord makes the pipe of His grace to flow into the marketplace, yet He expects His people to bring their pitchers there to get them filled. He spreads the table, but He does not force the food into our mouths. We must come to the table and eat of what He has prepared. He is liberal and gracious. There is more than enough to fill your every need. He will give grace, but we must go to Him for it in His own appointed way.

Before we close upon this first promised blessing, *Who is it that gives grace?* We are back to the spot from where we started. "*He* will give grace." Oh! I want so to make every believer cling to his God. He will give grace. You will not get grace from out of your own self. It will never spring up from within us apart from God. You will not get grace merely by using the means of grace as some try by mechanically having their morning prayer or going to public worship or reading their Bible chapter and feeling quite satisfied. No! You must get to God who gives grace, for no one else can. And what a blessing it is that you do not need anyone to help you come to Him! You can approach Him yourself through Jesus Christ, and He has promised by Himself to give you grace. You will not get it by working and praying in yourself, but if your mind can get right to the invisible God and ask Him for grace, He will give it. No one has ever sincerely sought the grace of God and not had it sooner or later. A man may be a long time seeking, but though the promise tarry, wait for it. It will come. God is faithful to His promise and will in due time answer your prayer. "He will give grace." Do not blot the promise out of your heart but cling and hang on to it as a drowning man clings to a plank.

God Will Give Glory

"He will give grace and glory." The word *and* may seem very insignificant, but in this case we would not take ten thousand dollars for these three letters. God has riveted the two things together, grace and glory. There are many who would like to take that diamond rivet out, but they cannot. The Lord does not say that He will give grace and perdition, and He does not say that He will give glory without first giving grace. He says He gives the two together.

If we have grace, we shall as surely have glory, for the two are tied up in one bundle. These are twin stars that shine together, and if you have shared His grace, His glory cannot be denied. Grace shall flower into glory as the bulb in the blossom. Grace shall rise as the fountain, and glory shall be its spreading river.

If we possess grace, we shall not perish, but if we have it not, we must perish and never know the glory. It is not possible that those shall be glorified who have not first of all been justified and then sanctified. Where grace does not reign in our hearts, we shall not reign in heaven.

"He shall give grace and glory." The glory that He shall give, how we need power to see it and understand it! "Eye hath not seen, nor ear heard, neither have entered into the heart of man, the things which God hath prepared for them that love him. But God hath revealed them unto us by his Spirit. . . . that we might know the things that are freely given to us of God" (1 Cor. 2:9–12). We do, therefore, know a little of what that glory is. The eye does not, the ear does not, but the enlightened soul taught of the Spirit of God does know what the glory will be. We know without a doubt that the glory we are to receive is *the glory of heaven*. Whatever heaven may be; whatever may be meant by the streets of shining gold, the gates of pearl, the walls of jasper and calcedony and sapphire; whatever may be indicated by crowns and palms and harps of gold; whatever may be signified by the river of the water of life and trees that bear twelve types of fruit for the healing of the nations—all this in perfection is the inheritance of those who have grace in their hearts. Oh, you shall have the harps! You shall wave the palms before your King! You shall sit down with Abraham, Isaac, and Jacob in the kingdom of God! If there are degrees of glory, as some say, yet it is very certain that the very least of the saints will have glory, and I do not see how the very greatest could have more.

The very doorkeepers, if there is such a position in the house of the Lord above, will have glory. I am sure we can say of heaven that if we may but have the lowest place there, we will bless the Lord to all eternity. The glory that God can give is the glory of heaven.

In the next place, it is *the glory of eternity*. Eternity! How do we begin to speak the word we do not know how to speak! Eternity! Eternity! Eternity! It must expound itself. We are always confusing it with time and speaking of the "countless ages of eternity" as though there were any "ages" or could be anything like counting in eternity at all. Eternity is of unending duration.

The glory that Christ is to give us will be such a glory as that. It will know no pause, never near to a conclusion, never decline, and we shall never grow weary of it, nor will it be weary of us. It is the glory of eternity.

Further, we are told by the Lord that the glory that He will give His people is *the glory of Christ*. "The glory which thou gavest me I have given them" (John 17:22). Can you imagine how glorious Christ is, not only in His nature originally, but now that He has obtained as a reward a seat upon His Father's throne? Whatever glory Jesus may have, He will share it with us, when we shall be like Him, and when we shall see Him as He is. It is the glory of Christ.

And to crown it all, *it is the glory of the Father Himself*, for Christ partakes in His Father's glory, and even so shall we. Does not your heart long and pant to know by actual enjoyment what this glory is? Oh, to get away from looking in the glass dimly and to finally glimpse the face of Christ! To have the clouds and mist all swept away, and in the serene atmosphere of heaven to behold the King in His beauty and the land that is very far off!

This glory is *the glory of perfect nature*—spotless, sinless, incorruptible; a body that can know no weakness or sickness or decay; a soul that will not be capable of temptation, that cannot be fretted by care nor distracted by trouble!

It is *the glory of victory*. The glory that God will give His people is the glory of bruising Satan under His feet, the glory of seeing the sword and the shield of the devil forever broken in pieces. It is the glory of seeing all the hosts of hell confounded and put to eternal shame by every one of the saints in whom Christ shall reign forever.

It is *the glory of perfect rest, perfect happiness, and perfect security*. It is the glory of pure blessedness. He who knows what it is when the whole soul shall be as full of happiness as it can hold, shall float, swim, dive, and plunge into seas of heavenly rest. It shall not be possible for a person there to have a wish ungratified or a desire unfulfilled. Every power shall find its fullest expression without weariness, and every passion shall have full indulgence without so much as a fear of sin.

The text says, "He will *give* glory." So, then, although glory is a reward and is often called so, yet still it is a gift. The rewards of grace are of grace. They are not legal rewards given to us because we deserve them. Christ first gives His servants grace to serve Him and then rewards them as if they had served Him in their own strength, though their service is His work in them rather than their work for Him. There is not a soul in heaven that came there by merit. There is not a note of self-righteousness to mar the song of free grace before the throne. It is all love, undeserved love, love without limit, love to be extolled throughout eternity.

But *when will He give glory*? If you have grown to manhood or womanhood, you will have it before seventy years from now. That is not very long, and that is if you live to old age. Some of you will reach the land of glory very soon. Others may be spared a little longer, but what is the difference in the time? It really seems to be no measurement at all. Life on earth is incredibly short compared with eternity. When we get to heaven, we shall wonder that we thought anything about time at all. An hour with our God will make up for all life's troubles. I suppose that one sight of Christ will take away all the taste of the bitters of life forever. We shall wonder why we ever fretted and worried ourselves with such little things as they were, such insignificant trifles. We will wonder how our light afflictions, which were but for a moment and are not worthy to be compared to the eternal weight of glory, should have exercised such a depressing influence upon our spirits at times.

We shall come to glory *when our work is done*. We shall not be kept from the wage a moment after it is earned. We shall come to glory when we are ready for it. When the fruit is mellow, the farmer gathers it in. Some grow mellow quickly, but some are long in the process. We shall get to heaven when we have really been tried in the furnace till there is no more need for the trying, when we have passed through the last crucible and have come out wholly sanctified, the process being complete.

We shall go to heaven *just when God has purposed it*. The devil with all the hosts of hell cannot keep us back a moment longer than that. We shall go there just when heaven will be most heaven to us. We shall go there just when we should have chosen to go ourselves, if we had had the wisdom of God to choose for us. We shall go there just when Christ will be ready to welcome us and when we shall know that He has prepared a place for us. Let us be patient then, and let us only hang hard upon this gracious promise: "He will give grace and glory."

*H*ere our English is a poor language as compared with the Greek, and I believe that Paul groaned when he wrote the matchless Greek of the text because even it could not express all his meaning. What if I read the phrase, "the hyperbolical wealth of grace" or "the superabounding, excessive, overflowing riches of the grace of God"? If I were to heap up epithets, I could not give you all that Paul means. But notice, first, that the riches of the grace of God are above all limit. God has as much grace as you could ever want, and He has a great deal more than that. The Lord has as much grace as a whole universe will require, but He has vastly more. He overflows. All the demands that can ever be made on the grace of God will never impoverish Him or even diminish His store of mercy. There will remain an incalculably precious mine of mercy as full as when he first began to bless the sons of men. God is so rich in mercy that you cannot tell how rich He is. His are overflowing riches, marvelous riches, exceeding riches. He is boundless in all His attributes, but emphatically so in His love.

Chapter Six

The Exceeding Riches of Grace

That in the ages to come he might shew the exceeding riches of his grace in his kindness toward us through Christ Jesus— Ephesians 2:7.

FROM THIS VERSE IT IS CLEAR that Paul fully expected the gospel of the grace of God to be preached in the ages to come. He had no notion of a temporary gospel to develop into a better one, but he was assured that the same gospel would be preached to the end of the dispensation. And I take it that Paul was stating that eternity itself will not improve upon the gospel. When all the saints are gathered home, they shall still speak of the wonders of Jehovah's love in Christ Jesus, and in the golden streets they shall stand up and tell what the Lord has done for them to listening crowds of angels and principalities and powers. Paul expected that throughout the ages to come the gospel would burn on with the same brilliance.

Paul looked upon these Ephesians newly drawn out from the slough of idolatry in the same light as he looked upon himself when he said that the Lord had shown all longsuffering toward him for an example to them that should afterward believe on Christ's name (1 Tim. 1:16). They were but types of what God can do by the gospel and what He will continue to do until the present dispensation is closed. We may gather with an assured logic that the gospel is altogether unalterable. Paul held it forth that the same results would follow in all ages from the preaching of the same gospel with the same power from heaven. Hold on to that original gospel, for it can never disappoint or fail.

Learn also from this language of Paul that every age is a gainer by those that preceded it. Whereas in the second century, men could only refer to the experience of saints during one hundred years, we now have the accumulated personal testimonies of twenty centuries of believers. Every year and every day has brought fresh trophies to its power, producing evidence of its divine power. We have no need to wonder whether this bread is good to eat or whether we dare ford the stream. These twenty centuries the hosts of God have gone through the flood in safety, and we have but to join their ranks and follow where they lead the way. Surrounded by evidence that is overwhelming, we behold the gospel of Jesus going forth, conquering and to conquer. We hear from ten thousand times ten thousand voices the cry, "Christ is the power of God and the wisdom of God." We cannot cease to proclaim the mercy of God as displayed in the atoning sacrifice of our Lord Jesus, for infallible assurances strengthen our confidence and set our hearts on fire. Thus is God's purpose in the text accomplished, that to the ages to come should be made known by all who have tasted of His kindness the exceeding riches of His grace toward men in Christ Jesus.

As I consider the text, I am utterly unable to express myself by reason of joyous astonishment. I feel as if I must sit down and lose myself in adoration. Here is a vast and fruitful country, a land of hills and valleys, a land of fountains and brooks of water. Who shall spy it out and then set its bounds? I will try to show one part of this, but the whole land I cannot show you. You must journey there for yourself. It is a royal subject: "the exceeding riches of his grace in his kindness toward us through Christ Jesus."

The Kindness of the Lord

What kindness Christ displayed in *choosing such sinners* as we were. These Ephesians had been most superstitious idolaters.

You recall how loudly they shouted, "Great is Diana of the Ephesians" (Acts 19:28). There was no preparedness in them to cast away their idols and to worship the great Invisible. There was nothing in them to draw them toward the light that shines in the Christ of God. They were far off, as Paul says, having no hope and really and truly without God in the world (Eph. 2:12–13). Yet these were the very ones whom the exceeding riches of God's grace brought out of darkness into marvelous light. They were "dead in trespasses and sins; wherein in time past ye walked according to the course of this world, according to the prince of the power of the air . . . fulfilling the desires of the flesh and and of mind; and were by nature the children of wrath" (Eph. 2:1–3). Yet the grace of God came to them and called out a church in Ephesus to show forth the praises of God.

Now, what are we? We may not have been sunk in the idolatry of Ephesus, but we were all sinners in some fashion. All the sheep went astray, though each followed a different downward road. We have fulfilled the lusts of the flesh and of the mind. We have had the same strong will and firm purpose that are the qualities under the devil's influence to soon force us down a passage to hell. If we had been left to sow our wild oats, what a crop we should have had by now. Thanks be to God for His preventing love! Some have wandered far and plunged deeply into sin, yet what a wonder of grace and miracle of love that God should have selected them and brought them near to Himself. Always recall what you would have been if it had not been for the kindness of God toward you in Christ Jesus. And recall that the Lord has shown this kindness so that others like us may be induced to believe in the same kindness. No doctrine, however clearly stated, will ever have such influence over others as living examples. When we tell our story of God's mercy to us, we in effect say to others, "Come, and you will not be refused. Leave your sin as we have done. Trust in Jesus, and you will find the same mercy for your salvation." It is delightful to dwell on the word "his kindness toward *us*."

But our attention is called not only to the persons whom God chose but also to His kindness displayed in *the gracious acts that He has shown toward them*. Mark the exceeding riches of His grace in His kindness toward us. He chose us before He lit the stars. He wrote our names upon the heart and hands of Christ before He laid the foundations of the hills. In the fullness of time He gave Christ for us, even that blessed Christ of whom we say, "Who loved me, and gave himself for me" (Gal. 2:20). He made a covenant with us in Christ Jesus that shall stand when all created things dissolve. Having done this, He watched over us when we were bondslaves to the tyrant Satan. Graciously He guarded us from going further still into transgression and committing the sin that is unto death. Then He called us, and when we would not come, He drew us yet more forcibly by His effectual grace. Then He washed us and made us whiter than snow. He brought us the best robe and put it on us and made us lovely in His sight. He gave us the kiss of sweet acceptance and put us among His children and deals with us in His love. We have been guided, led, instructed, upheld, and sanctified, and the almighty Savior is still performing for us miracles of mercy. He has made a pathway for us that we may ascend to the right hand of God, even the Father, and sit in the heavenly places with Christ. What has He not done? What more could He do? Oh, the goodness, the manifold goodness, the overflowing, surpassing, inconceivable goodness of God in His kindness toward us through Christ Jesus!

I am bound to dwell a moment on that last phrase: His kindness toward us *through Christ Jesus*. That is the channel through which all blessing has come to us. God gives common mercies to men as His creatures, but these riches of His grace come to us as His chosen through the Mediator. You can see the mark of the cross on every spiritual blessing that the Father has bestowed. It seems to make every covenant blessing more and more dear because it was brought to us by the hand of the Beloved. By His atonement it is procured to us, and by His matchless intercession it is actually bestowed. All things come to us through Christ Jesus. He is the golden pipe of the conduit of eternal love, the window through which grace shines, the door by which it enters. Turn these words over and over in your soul and see if there is not the very music of heaven sleeping within them that your faith may call forth and coin into hallelujahs. "The exceeding riches of his grace in his kindness toward us in Christ Jesus"—this is an anthem worthy of the celestial choirs. Sing it, O you chosen of the Lord, while you are waiting to ascend His holy hill.

The Exceeding Riches of His Grace

Here our English is a poor language as compared with the Greek, and I believe that Paul groaned when he wrote the matchless Greek of the text because even it could not express all his meaning. What if I read the phrase, "the hyperbolical wealth of grace" or "the superabounding, excessive, overflowing riches of the grace of God"? If I were to heap up epithets, I could not give you all that Paul means. But notice, first, that the riches of the grace of God are *above all limit*. God has as much grace as you could ever want, and He has a great deal more than that. The Lord has as much grace as a whole universe will require, but He has vastly more. He overflows. All the demands that can ever be made on the grace of God will never impoverish Him or even diminish His store of mercy. There will remain an incalculably precious mine of mercy as full as when he first began to bless the sons of men. God is so rich in mercy that you cannot tell how rich He is. His are overflowing riches, marvelous riches, exceeding riches. He is boundless in all His attributes, but emphatically so in His love.

His grace is *above all observation*. The little grace that you have seen bears no proportion to the glorious whole. It is like the man standing on the beach at Brighton who thinks he sees the sea. No one has ever beheld to the full the vast, majestic ocean in all its length and breadth and depth. No one can see it in all its far resounding shores and hollow caves. Such is the "exceeding riches" of God's grace—unsearchable, passing knowledge. My poor pen and dull language are left behind. It overflows my soul and drowns my speech, but you must consider it for yourself. The grace of God surpasses all you know, all you see, and all you think.

So I remark next that this grace is *above all expression*, even inspired expression. Paul, though full of the Holy Spirit, could not speak out all the love of God in Christ Jesus, for His love is unspeakable. "Thanks be unto God for his unspeakable gift" (2 Cor. 9:15). If we had all the tongues of men and of angels, we could not declare all the riches of the grace of God. No. If all the orators that ever lived made this their one and only theme, and if all of them were under the influence of the divine Spirit, still human language could not compass this divine thing. If we knew the language of angels, we could not even then declare the grace of God. The most experienced saints bewail the weakness of every form of speech to describe it.

We are compelled to add that it is *above all our ways of action.* The gospel has taught us to forgive, but we do not take to it naturally. If anyone treats us poorly, it is with some difficulty that we forgive. And if we do forgive, we do not always forget. But such is the greatness of God's mercy that we who have wearied ourselves and Him with our sin, yet we have not outworn His compassion. God delights to pardon: "he delighteth in mercy" (Mic. 7:18). Twenty-six times in one psalm the sweet singer proclaims that "his mercy endureth forever" (Ps. 136). How he rings that bell again and again and again. Your mercy is very short, and your temper is quick so that you speak angrily very soon, but it is not so with God. So wondrous are His ways of grace that they are past finding out. We cannot follow them and can hardly believe them because they are so unlike ours. His ways are above our ways, and His thoughts above our thoughts, as much as the heavens are above the earth (Isa. 55:9). The gentlest, meekest, and most loving minds are left far behind in this race of love. Our little stream of goodness runs after much pumping and pressure, but the river of divine love flows freely on.

And the ways of grace are *above our understanding.* Some famous minds have been born into the world now and then, men who have explored the sun, threaded the stars, and pried into the depths of the earth. God raises up now and then masterminds to perceive and reveal His wisdom in nature. But there never was or shall be a human understanding that can fully grasp the incomprehensible riches of the mercy of God in Christ Jesus. I have barely touched it with a swallow's wing; I have not dived into the fathomless depths, nor can I. Jehovah is such a marvelously forgiving God, so rich in His mercy that our understanding cannot count the mighty sum. If our thoughts were raised to the utmost and our hearts so pure that we could see God, not even then could we know all the exceeding riches of His grace to us who believe. The loftiest thought of the most saintly mind never rose to the height of this argument. The most masterly poetic conception faints, its wing droops, and it falls to earth in the presence of this mercy that is higher than the heavens.

Furthermore, the exceeding riches of God's grace may be guessed at by the fact that divine mercy is *above all our sins*. You cannot sin so much as God can forgive. If it comes to a battle between sin and grace, you shall never be so bad as God shall be good. You can only sin as a man, but God can forgive as a God. You sin as a finite creature, but the Lord forgives as the infinite Creator. When that thought struck my soul last night, I felt like Abraham when he laughed for joy. I sin like a man, but He forgives like a God. We will never sin that grace may abound, for that is detestable. But what a blessed text it is: "Where sin abounded, grace did much more abound" (Rom. 5:20). Gross and intolerable as your sin may be, yet it is but as the drop of a bucket compared with the immense ocean of forgiving love. Does not this magnify the mercy of God?

Try again. God's mercy is *greater than His promises*. "But," you say, "we have read of 'exceeding great and precious promises.'" I tell you His mercy has a glory beyond His promises, for His mercy is the father of His promises. The Lord had mercy and grace before He had spoken a single promise. It was because His heart was flaming with love that He made a covenant of grace and wrote therein the words of peace. His promises are precious streams that come leaping up in the deserts of our lost and ruined state, but the depth that lies under is richer than the fountain that comes out of it. The mercy of God as the source is greater than the promises that flow from it and infinitely greater than our limited interpretations of the promises that fall far short of their real meaning.

God's mercy is *greater than all that all His children ever have received as yet*. His redeemed are a multitude that no man can number, and each one draws heavily from the source of grace, yet there is more grace in God than He has given as yet. We make a mistake if we think that His mercy is all given out in this life. Much of His mercy is laid up for enjoyment in the world to come. The Lord has prepared for them that love Him an inconceivable bliss. There is heaven, there is glory, there is all the bliss of the endless ages yet laid up in store. Oh, the wealth of these heavenly reserves! There will be no possibility of draining the wondrous flood of mercy that comes flowing from the throne of God. God's ability to give is greater than our capacity to receive.

The fact is that this grace is *above all measure*. It is higher than our sin, though that be exceedingly heinous and proudly threatens the gates of heaven. It is higher than our thoughts, though our imagination sometimes takes a condor's flight. Oh, the height of divine mercy! It rises to the throne of the Eternal. As for the depths of grace, while the sea has immense depths, the mercy of God is altogether unfathomable. Great sins sink into it and are lost, but grace is just as deep after it has swallowed up a world's sin as it was before. There are inconceivably deep places in God's mercy where the blackest sins are lost. Out of these come the choicest pearls of grace. Oh, the depths! As for the breadth of mercy, David said, "As far as the east is from the west, so far hath he removed our transgressions from us" (Ps. 103:12). What greater breadth can be conceived? As for the length of it, it is from everlasting to everlasting. Can anyone tell me the length of that? My sins began less than fifty years ago, but the Lord's mercy began—ah, when did it begin? It was always with Him, and His plans of mercy are from everlasting. There is a beginning to man's sin, but there is no beginning to pardoning love. Who can compass a matter that in any one of the measurements far surpasses all human computation? Grace is above all calculation.

Let us come, then, let us come. However much we may have wandered and however defiled, God delights in mercy. Do not dishonor my Lord by measuring your sin and affirming that it outstrips His mercy. It cannot be! You know nothing about the glorious nature of my Lord. A child may fill its little cup out of the sea, but the sea never misses it. Your sin is like that cup, and you may fill it to the brim with mercy, but the ocean of love will never miss all that you can take from it. Come, take all that you can take, and no one shall question you. Wash out your crimson stains in this pure flood, and it shall remain as pure as at the first. I would not speak lightly of your sin, but still I do say over again that as compared with the infinite mercy of God it is but as a shadow to the sun or a grain of sand to the full ocean.

Still More Grace

What exceeding riches of grace it was on God's part that when we resisted Him in the days of our sin *He resolved to overcome our folly.* The Lord pleads with sinners to accept His grace: "Come now, and let us reason together, saith the LORD" (Isa. 1:18). He begs and beseeches men that they will be saved, entreating, pleading, and arguing with them that they would turn to Jesus and live. That is an exceeding riches of grace. He stands waiting, waiting long, knocking at our door, though we would not let Him in. But He would not take no for an answer.

The exceeding riches of His grace were seen in *making no conditions with us.* When the Lord Jesus met us, He did not stand out for terms. I heard someone say the other day, "I do not feel enough brokenness of heart." Who said that Christ demanded so much brokenness of heart or so much humbling of spirit before He would give His mercy? Christ comes to you just as you are, in all your alienation and enmity, and brings everything in His hands that you can want. That is what we call free grace. There was nothing in us to draw Christ to us. He saw us lying by the roadside bruised and broken, and He did not say, "Come, poor man; rise up, and I will bind your wounds." No. He came where we were lying unable to stir and poured in the wine and oil and did it all without our help. This is the "exceeding riches of his grace" of freely giving us all we need, only asking that we would receive it, that we would be empty, and that He might fill us with His love.

I think I never knew "the exceeding riches of his grace" better than when I thought *how His grace works.* He does all this with a word. He speaks a dead sinner into life with a word. "Live," He says, and the dead one lives. He who had been accounted un-righteous is reckoned righteous by God's will, and He is righteous for those whom God reckons to be righteous, by the imputation of Christ's righteousness are righteous indeed.

If you want further proof of "the exceeding riches," consider the power of the blood. Once washed in the crimson fount, your every sin is gone, every spot is washed out, and gone never to return. He that is once washed in the atoning blood will never be dirty again. The cleansing is perfected forever. The glorious High Priest made one offering for sin, only one. He did it once, and by that He annihilated all the sins of His people at a single stroke, once for all. His word and His blood have wrought such wondrous mysteries of grace.

Have not "the exceeding riches of his grace" been marvelous to you? To think that He should accept us as believers though we had no more than half a grain of faith! He has even treated us as believers when sometimes we have been more doubters than trusters. As for our repentance, it seemed such a poor shallow regret, yet He has reckoned it repentance. Our poor love to Him has been like a spark hiding away in the ashes, yet He has called it love. He has known us better than we know ourselves, and He has known we loved Him notwithstanding the feebleness of our affection. These poor, frail graces of ours that we have been ashamed of, He has nevertheless rejoiced in them and had a joy in them as being the gift of His Spirit.

And since our conversion the Lord has *held on to us* and helped us hold on to Him. We have tried Him sorely time after time. Sometimes we talk about our trials. There is another side of that. Think of Christ's trials, and how we have grieved Him. We must have provoked His Spirit ten thousand times, yet He loves us infinitely and does not give us up. He has not grown cold in His love; notwithstanding our chilliness He loves us now with all His great and infinite heart.

But when we get to heaven, we shall truly be amazed at the mercy that He will then be giving us at His right hand. We may as well give up the endless task of trying to understand its sum. The Lord will go on to deluge us with mercy, grace, favor, forever and ever. We shall say to one another, when millions of years have gone by, "Brother, is it still not astonishing? I know far more of the grace of God now, but I am as far off as ever from knowing all of it, for now I know more of my ignorance. I only know more of the extent of what I do not know."

You cannot get ahold of salvation by grace by any other means than by faith. This live coal from God's altar needs the golden tongs of faith with which to carry it. Salvation in our case means a deliverance from guilt and ruin, and this could not happen by our doing a measure of good works, since we are not in a condition to perform any. And if we did have to perform works for salvation, salvation would have soon appeared to be of debt and not altogether of grace. Salvation by grace can only be gripped by the hand of faith. The attempt to lay hold upon it by the doing of certain acts of law would cause the grace to evaporate. Grace is not grace if works are mixed in.

Chapter Seven

All of Grace

For by grace are ye saved through faith; and that not of your-selves: it is the gift of God—Ephesians 2:8.

THESE WORDS OF THE APOSTLE PAUL contain the sum of my theology and preaching over the years as regards the salvation of men. It is a text that also closely connects me with my grandfather. It is now many years ago when I was to preach in a country town in one of the eastern counties. It is rare for me to be late, but due to railway delays I arrived at the chapel considerably behind the time. Like sensible people, they had begun their worship and proceeded as far as the sermon. As I neared the chapel, I perceived that someone was in the pulpit preaching, and who should the preacher be but my dear and venerable grandfather! He saw me as I came in the front door. At once he said, "Here comes my grandson! He may preach the gospel better than I can, but he cannot preach a better gospel; can you, Charles?" As I made my way up the aisle, I answered, "You can preach better than I can. Pray go on." But he would not agree to *that*. He said, "I was preaching on 'For by grace are ye saved.' I have been setting forth the source and fountainhead of salvation, and I am now showing them the channel of it, through faith.

Now you take it up, and go on." And so I did, taking off right where he had stopped.

I was so much at home with these glorious truths that I could not feel any difficulty in taking from my grandfather the thread of his message and joining my thread to it, so as to continue without a break. We so agreed on the things of God that when I proceeded to the next point on the weakness and inability of human nature, "and that not of yourselves," my beloved grandsire pulled on my coat and took his turn again. The good old man said, "When I spoke of our depraved human nature, I know most about that, dear friends." And so he took up the parable and for five minutes set forth a solemn and humbling description of our lost estate, the depravity of our nature, and the spiritual death under which we were found. Finishing that, I was allowed to go on again to the dear old man's great delight. Now and then he would say in a gentle tone, "Good! Good!" Once he said, "Tell them that again, Charles," and, of course, I did tell them *that* again. While reading this verse, I seem to hear that dear voice, which has been so long lost to earth, saying to me, "Tell them that again." If my grandfather could return to earth, he would find me where he left me, steadfast in the faith and true to that doctrine that was once delivered to the saints.

There Is a Present Salvation

The apostle says, "Ye are saved." Not "ye shall be" or "ye may be" but "ye are saved." He does not say, "Ye are partly saved" or "ye hope to be saved." Let us be as clear on this point as Paul was, and let us never rest until we know that we are saved. At this moment we are either saved or unsaved. That is clear. I hope that by the witness of the Holy Spirit we may be so assured of our standing as to sin. "The LORD is my strength and song, and is become my salvation" (Ps. 118:14).

A Present Salvation Must Be Through Grace

There is no other present salvation except that which begins and ends with "by grace are ye saved." Many preach salvation by works, but where works are involved, salvation must come at a future time. The works being unfinished, the salvation is incomplete. If salvation is complete, the main motive of the legalist would be gone.

Salvation must be by grace. If man is lost by sin, how can he be saved except through the grace of God? If man stands under condemnation, how can he reverse that by himself? Suppose that he should keep the law perfectly the rest of his life, he will then have done only what he was always bound to have done. What is to become of the past? How can old sins and ruin be blotted out. Common sense and Scripture tell us that salvation can be only through the free favor of God.

People may contend for salvation by works, but you will not hear anyone support his own argument by saying, "I am myself saved by what I have done." That would be a superabundance of arrogance that few people would go to. Pride could hardly compass itself about with such extravagant boasting. No, if we are saved, it must be by the favor of God. No one professes to be an example of the opposite view.

Salvation to be complete must be by free favor. When the saints come to die, they never conclude their lives by hoping in their good works. I have never stood by the bedside of a godly man who reposed any confidence whatever in his own prayers or repentance or spirituality. I have heard eminently holy saints quoting in death the words, "Christ Jesus came into the world to save sinners" (1 Tim. 1:15). In fact, the nearer believers come to heaven, the most simple is their trust in the merit of the Lord Jesus and the more intensely do they abhor all trust in themselves. If this is true in our last moments, when the conflict is almost over, much more should we feel it to be so while we are in the thick of the fight. If a man is completely saved in this present time of warfare, how can it be except by grace? While he has to confess innumerable shortcomings and sin mixed with all he does, how can he believe that he is completely saved except by the free favor of God?

Paul speaks of this salvation as belonging to the Ephesians: "By grace are *ye* saved." Despite the past covenant the Ephesians had with the powers of darkness through curious arts and works of divination (Acts 19:19), they were said to be possessors of salvation. If such as these are saved, it must be all of grace. I know it is so in my own case, and I believe it is a rule that holds true for all believers.

Present Salvation by Grace Must Be Through Faith

You cannot get ahold of salvation by grace by any other means than by faith. This live coal from God's altar needs the golden tongs of faith with which to carry it. Salvation in our case means a deliverance from guilt and ruin, and this could not happen by our doing a measure of good works, since we are not in a condition to perform any. And if we did have to perform works for salvation, salvation would have soon appeared to be of debt and not altogether of grace. Salvation by grace can only be gripped by the hand of faith. The attempt to lay hold upon it by the doing of certain acts of law would cause the grace to evaporate. Grace is not grace if works are mixed in.

Some try to lay hold upon salvation by grace through the use of ceremonies, but it will not do. You are christened, are confirmed, and receive "the holy sacrament" from priestly hands, or you are baptized, join the church, and sit at the Lord's table. Does this bring salvation? I ask you, "Have you salvation?" You dare not say yes. If you did claim salvation of a sort, yet I am sure it would not be in your mind salvation by grace.

Others try to lay hold upon salvation by grace through their feelings. The hand of faith is constructed for the grasping of a present salvation by grace, but feeling is not adapted for that end. If you say, "I must feel that I am saved. I must feel so much sorrow and so much joy, or else I will not know that I am saved," you will find that this method will not work. You might as well hope to see with your ear or taste with your eye or hear with your nose as to believe by feeling. Feeling is the wrong organ. After you have believed, you can enjoy salvation by feeling its heavenly influences. But to dream of getting a grasp of it by your feelings is as foolish as attempting to carry away the sunlight in the palm of your hand.

Moreover, the evidence produced by feeling is singularly fickle. When your feelings are peaceful and delightful, they are soon broken in upon and become restless and melancholy. The least thing may sink or raise our spirits. Experienced believers come to think less and less of their present emotions as they reflect upon the little reliance that can be safely placed upon them. Faith receives the statement of God concerning His way of gracious pardon, and thus it brings salvation to the believer. But warm feelings from passionate appeals, yielding yourself deliriously to a hope that you dare not examine, whirling around in a sort of dervish dance of excitement that has become necessary for its own sustaining, is all on a stir, like the troubled sea that cannot rest. From its boilings and ragings, feeling is apt to drop to lukewarmness, despondency, despair, and all the kindred evils. Feelings are a set of cloudy, windy phenomena that cannot be trusted in reference to the eternal truths of God.

Salvation by Grace Through Faith
Is Not of Ourselves

The salvation, the faith, and the whole gracious work together are not of ourselves.

First, they are *not of our past good endeavors.* No unregenerate person has lived so well that God is bound to give him further grace and to bestow on him eternal life. Salvation is given *to* us, not earned *by* us. Our past life is always a wandering away from God. Our new life of return to God is always a work of undeserved mercy.

It is not of ourselves in that it is *not out of our original excellence.* Salvation comes from above. It is never evolved from within. Can eternal life be evolved from the bare ribs of death? Some dare to say that faith in Christ and the new birth are only the development of good things that lay hidden in us by nature. But in this, like their father, they speak of their own. If an heir of wrath is left to be developed, he will become more and more fit for the place prepared for the devil and his angels! You may educate the unregenerate man to the highest, but he remains and must forever remain dead in sin unless a higher power shall come in to save him from himself. Grace brings into the heart an entirely foreign element. It does not improve and perpetuate, but it kills and makes alive. There is no continuity between the state of nature and the state of grace. The one is darkness, and the other is light. The one is death, and the other is life. When grace comes to us, it is like a firebrand dropped into the sea, where it would certainly be quenched were it not of such a miraculous quality that it baffles the waters and sets up its reign of fire and light even in the depths.

Salvation by grace through faith is not of ourselves *in the sense of being the result of our own power.* We are abound to view salvation as being as surely a divine act as creation or providence or resurrection. At every point of the process of salvation, this phrase is appropriate: *"not of yourselves."* From the first desire after it to the full reception of it by faith, it is evermore of the Lord alone and not of ourselves. The man believes, but that belief is only one result among many of the implantation of divine life within the man's soul by God Himself.

Even the very will to be saved by grace is not of ourselves but is the gift of God. A man should believe in Jesus. It is his duty to receive Him whom God has set forth to be a propitiation for sins. But many will not believe. Unless the Spirit of God convinces the judgment and constrains the will, man has no heart to believe in Jesus unto eternal life. I ask any saved person to look back upon his conversion and explain how it came about. You turned to Christ and believed in His name. These were your own acts and deeds. But what caused you to turn? What sacred power was that which turned you from sin to righteousness? Do you attribute this singular renewal to the existence of something better in you than has been yet discovered in your unconverted neighbor? No. You confess that you might be what he is now if it had not been that there was a potent something that touched the spring of your will, enlightened your understanding, and guided you to the foot of the cross. Gratefully we confess the fact; it must be so. None of us will dream of taking any honor to ourselves from our conversion or from any gracious effect that has flowed from the first divine cause.

It Is the Gift of God

Salvation may be truly traced to its source in the gift unspeakable: the free, unmeasured blessing of God's love. Salvation is *the gift of God in opposition to a wage*. When a man pays another his wage, he is only doing what is right. But we praise God for salvation because it is not the payment of debt but is the gift of grace. No man enters eternal life on earth or in heaven as his due. It is the gift of God. Salvation is so purely, so absolutely, a gift of God that nothing can be more free. God gives it because He chooses to give it of His own sovereign grace. This is His holy prerogative.

Salvation is *the gift of God: that is to say completely so, in opposition to the notion of growth*. Salvation is not a natural production from within. It is brought from a foreign zone and planted within the heart by heavenly hands. Salvation is in its entirety a gift from God. If you will have it, there it is complete. Will you have it as a perfect gift? "No. I will produce it in my own workshop." You cannot forge a work so rare and costly upon which even Jesus gave His lifeblood. Here is a garment without seam, woven from the top throughout. It will cover you and make you glorious. Will you have it? "No. I will sit at the loom and weave clothing of my own." Only a proud fool does that. He spins cobwebs and weaves a dream. Oh, to freely take what Christ upon the cross declared to be finished!

It is *the gift of God: that is, it is eternally secure in opposition to the gifts of men that soon pass away*. "Not as the world giveth, give I unto you," says our Lord Jesus (John 14:27). If my Lord Jesus gives you salvation at this moment, *you have it*, and you have it forever. He will never take it back again. And if He does not take it from you, who can? If He saves you *now* through faith, you are saved—so saved that you shall never perish, neither shall any pluck you out of His hand. May it be so with you!

When it is said that the doctrines of grace will create sin, I appeal to the facts and leave the oracle to answer as it may. If we are ever to see a pure and godly England where drunkenness and social evil have been put out, it must be by the proclamation of the grace of God. Men must be forgiven by grace, renewed by grace, transformed by grace, sanctified by grace, preserved by grace; and when that comes to pass, the golden age will dawn. But while men are only taught duty and left to their own strength, it is a labor in vain. You may flog a dead horse a long while before it will stir. To teach men to walk who have no feet is poor work, and such is instruction in morals before grace gives a heart to love holiness. The gospel alone supplies men with motive and strength, and therefore it is to the gospel we must look as the real reformer of men.

Chapter Eight

Doctrines of Grace
Do Not Lead to Sin

For sin shall not have dominion over you: for ye are not under the law, but under grace. What then? shall we sin, because we are not under the law, but under grace? God forbid—Romans 6:14–15.

THE SUBSTANCE AND THE ESSENCE of the true gospel are the doctrine of God's grace. If you take away the grace of God from the gospel, you have extracted from it its very lifeblood, and there is nothing left worth preaching, worth believing, worth contending for. Grace is the soul and the music of the gospel; without it, the gospel is silent.

The doctrine of grace teaches that God deals with sinful men upon the footing of pure mercy. Finding men guilty, out of free favor He has provided in the death of His dear Son an atonement that freely pardons men, altogether irrespective of past character or of any good works that may be foreseen. He accepts all those who place their trust in this atonement, selecting faith as the way of salvation, that it may be all of grace. In this God acts from a motive found with Himself. This grace of God flows toward the sinner from of old and begins its operations upon him when there is nothing good in him, working in him that which is good and acceptable and continuing so to work in him until the deed of grace is complete when the believer is received up into the glory for which he is made. Grace commences to save and perseveres till all is done. Everything in salvation is of grace, and grace alone. All is of free favor, nothing of merit. "For by grace are ye saved through faith; and that not of yourselves: it is the gift of God."

No sooner is this doctrine set forth in a clear light than men begin to object to it. It is the target for all carnal logic to shoot at. Unrenewed minds have never liked it and never will; it is so humbling to human pride, making so light of the nobility of human nature. That men must as condemned criminals receive pardon by the exercise of royal prerogative or else perish in their sins is a teaching they cannot endure. Rather than meekly touch the silver scepter of God's mercy and accept undeserved favor just because God wills to give it, they turn aside and fight against the empire of grace. The unrenewed mind seeks out artillery to fight against the gospel of grace, and one of the biggest guns he has ever brought to the front is the declaration that the doctrine of grace leads to licentiousness. If great sinners are freely forgiven, men will more readily become great sinners. And the unrenewed infer that if God's grace abides with redeemed sinners, they can be persuaded to live as they like and still be saved. I have heard this constantly repeated argument so many times that it wearies me with its vain and false noise. In part it is a great mistake arising from a misconception, and in part it is a great lie because men know better.

I begin by admitting that the charge does appear somewhat probable. It does seem likely that if we say, "The worst of sinners may be forgiven through believing in Jesus Christ," sin will seem to be a cheap thing. It does seem probable that some may basely say, "Let us sin without restraint, for we can easily obtain forgiveness." But what looks to be probable is not certain; on the contrary, the improbable and the unexpected often come to pass. In questions of moral influence, nothing is more deceptive than theory. The ways of the human mind are not to be laid down with a pencil and a compass. Even what looks logical is not always inevitable, for men's minds are not governed by rules of the schools. On the contrary, I assert that ungodly men do not as a rule plead the grace of God as an excuse for their sin. As a rule, they are too indifferent to care about reasons at all. If they do offer an excuse, it is usually more flimsy and superficial. There may be a few men of perverse minds who have used this argument, but there is no accounting for the freaks of the fallen understanding. I suspect that when it is put forward that it is a mere pretense and not a plea that has satisfied the sinner's own conscience. Most are too utterly ashamed to state the argument in plain terms. I question whether the devil himself would be found reasoning this way: "God is merciful; therefore, let us be more sinful." Surely no intelligent being can really persuade itself that the goodness of God is a reason for offending Him more than ever. Moral insanity produces strange reasonings, but it is my solemn conviction that very rarely do men practically consider the grace of God to be a motive for sin.

While a few people have turned the grace of God into lasciviousness, I trust that no one will ever argue against any doctrine on account of the perverse use of it. Every truth can be perverted. Is there a single biblical doctrine that graceless hands have not twisted into mischief? There is an almost infinite ingenuity in wicked men for making evil out of good. Let us act as rational men. We do not find fault with ropes because poor insane creatures have hanged themselves with it.

It may appear probable that the doctrine of free grace will be made into a license for sin, but a better acquaintance with the curious working of the human mind corrects the notion. Fallen as human nature is, it is still human and therefore does not take kindly to certain forms of evil—such as human ingratitude. It is hardly human to multiply injuries upon those who return continued benefits. It reminds me of the story of a half-dozen boys who had severe fathers who often beat them within an inch of their lives. Another boy was with them who was tenderly loved by his parents. These young men met together to discuss robbing a nearby orchard. They were all anxious to get at it, except for the favored boy who would not go along with it. One of the others cried, "*You* need not worry. If our fathers catch us, we shall be beaten, but your father won't lay a hand on *you*." The little boy answered, "And do you think that because my father is kind to me, therefore I will do wrong and grieve him? I will do nothing of the sort to my dear father." It appears that the argument of the many boys was not overpoweringly convincing to their companion. The opposite conclusion was quite as logical and evidently carried weight with it. If God is good to the undeserving, some men will go into sin, but there are others of a nobler order whom the goodness of God leads to repentance.

I cannot help observing that I have known persons object to the evil influence of the doctrines of grace who were by no means qualified by their own morality to be judges of the subject. Morals must be in a poor way when immoral persons become their guardians. A proper response to this lie is to ask, "What has morality to do with you, or you with it?" These sticklers for good works are not often the doers of them. Let legalists look to their own hands and tongues, leaving the gospel of grace and its advocates to answer for themselves.

Looking back in history, I see upon its pages a refutation of the oft-repeated defamation. Who dares to suggest that those who believed in the grace of God have been sinners above other sinners? I dare those who throw the stones to first prove themselves superior in character. When have the saints been the patrons of vice and the defenders of injustice? Did the Puritans pander to licentiousness or iniquity? In their day, it was the theological party that preached salvation by works whose speech was savored with profanity and whose conduct was bedabbled with lust and wantonness. The Puritans were found on their knees crying to God for help in temptation; and in persecuting times they might be found in prison, cheerfully suffering the loss of all things for the truth's sake. The Puritans were the godliest men on the face of the earth. Are men so inconsistent as to nickname them for their purity and yet say that their doctrines led to sin?

Nor are the Puritans the only instance of it. All history confirms this rule. When it is said that the doctrines of grace will create sin, I appeal to the facts and leave the oracle to answer as it may. If we are ever to see a pure and godly England where drunkenness and social evil have been put out, it must be by the proclamation of the grace of God. Men must be forgiven by grace, renewed by grace, transformed by grace, sanctified by grace, preserved by grace; and when that comes to pass, the golden age will dawn. But while men are only taught duty and left to their own strength, it is a labor in vain. You may flog a dead horse a long while before it will stir. To teach men to walk who have no feet is poor work, and such is instruction in morals before grace gives a heart to love holiness. The gospel alone supplies men with motive and strength, and therefore it is to the gospel we must look as the real reformer of men.

The doctrine of grace and the whole plan of salvation by grace is most promotive of holiness. Wherever it comes, it helps us to say, "God forbid," to the question, "Shall we sin, because we are not under the law, but under grace?" This I would set out in the clear sunlight.

Salvation from the Power of Sin

Some suppose that when we preach salvation to the vilest of men we mean a mere deliverance from hell and an entrance into heaven. It includes that and results in that, but that is not what we mean. What we mean by salvation is this—deliverance from the love of sin, rescue from the habit of sin, setting free from the desire to sin. If it is true that grace delivers from sin, in what way will that gift produce sin? I fail to see any danger there. On the contrary, I say to the man who proclaims a gracious promise of victory over sin, "Make all speed! Go up and down throughout the world and tell the vilest of mankind that God is willing by His grace to set them free from the love of sin and to make new creatures of them." The gospel never hints that the ungodly may by believing continue to enjoy their sins and escape punishment. The gospel says that the ungodly may by believing in the Lord Jesus be enabled to change those lives so that they shall live unto God instead of serving sin and Satan. Even the most dead, dry bones of a soul can be made to live by His Spirit. That renewal will be seen in holy thoughts and pure words and righteous acts to the glory of God. In great love God is prepared to work all these things in all who believe. What possible harm can come of it? I defy the most cunning adversary to object upon the ground of morals to God's giving men new hearts and right spirits even as He pleases.

Love Possesses a Great Power Over Men

In the infancy of history, nations dream that crime can be put down by severity and rely upon fierce punishments, but experience corrects the error. Our English forefathers dreaded forgery, which is a troubling fraud that interferes with the confidence that exists between men. To put it down, they made forgery a capital offense. Alas, for the murders committed by that law! Yet the constant use of the gallows was never sufficient to stamp out the crime. Many offenses have been created and multiplied by the penalty that was meant to suppress them. Some offenses have almost died out when the penalty against them has been lightened.

It is a notable fact that if men are forbidden to do a thing, they straightway desire to do it, though they may have never thought of doing it before. Law commands obedience but does not promote it. Law often creates disobedience, and too stiff a penalty has been known to provoke an offense. Law fails, but love wins.

Love in any case makes sin infamous. To steal from another is bad, but to steal from a friend who has often helped one in need is a disgraceful crime. Love brands sin on the forehead with a red-hot iron. To kill an enemy is a grievous offense, but to slay a father to whom he owes his life cries out like a hideous monster. In the light of love, sin is seen to be exceedingly sinful.

Nor is this all. *Love has a great constraining power toward the highest form of virtue.* Deeds that a man could not be compelled to do on the ground of law, men have cheerfully done because of love. Those who would revolt against being forced to risk their lives by law will freely do so to save their fellow men. "For scarcely for a righteous man will one die: yet peradventure for a good man some would even dare to die" (Rom. 5:7). Goodness wins the heart, and one is ready to die for the kind and generous.

Look how men have thrown their lives away for their leaders. That was an immortal saying of the wounded French soldier. When searching for the bullet, the surgeon cut deeply, and the patient cried out, "A little lower and you will touch the emperor." Duty holds the fort, but love casts its body in the way of a deadly bullet. Who would think of sacrificing his life on the ground of law? Love alone counts not life so dear as the service of the beloved. Love to Jesus creates a heroism of which law knows nothing. All the history of the church of Christ, when it has been true to its Lord, is a proof of this.

Kindness also, working by the law of love, has often changed the most unworthy and therein proved that it is not a factor of evil. A drunkard woke up one morning from his drunken sleep with his clothes on him just as he had rolled down the night before. He saw his only child, his daughter Millie, getting his breakfast. Coming to his senses, he asked, "Millie, why do you stay with me?" She answered, "Because you are my father, and because I love you." He looked at himself as the ragged, good-for-nothing creature that he was, and he answered her, "Millie, do you really love me?" The child replied, "Yes, Father, I do, and I will never leave you. Before mother died, she said, 'Millie, stick to your father and always pray for him. One of these days he will give up his drink and be a good father to you.' So I will never leave you." It is wonderful to add to the story that Millie's father cast away his drink and became a Christian man. Millie was trying free grace, was she not? According to our moralists, she should have said, "Father, you are a horrible wretch! I have stuck to you long enough. If I stay with you, I shall be encouraging other fathers to get drunk." But the power of love made a better man of him.

Hear another story. In the old persecuting times here in England, there lived a merchant who feared God and attended the secret meetings of the saints. Near him there dwelt a poor cobbler whose needs were often relieved by the merchant. But the poor man was evil-hearted and with hopes of a reward issued information against his friend on the score of religion. This accusation would have brought the merchant to death by burning if he had not found the means of escape. Returning to his house, the merchant did not change his generous behavior to the malignant cobbler but was more liberal than ever. The cobbler avoided the good man with all his might, running away at his reproach. One day he was obliged to meet him face to face, and the Christian man asked him gently, "Why do you shun me? I am not your enemy. I know all that you did to injure me, but I never had an angry thought against you. I have helped you, and I am willing to do so as long as I live, only let us be friends." Would you wonder that it was not long before the evil cobbler was subdued by the power of love and brought to Christ. Grace has a strange subduing power and leads men to goodness, drawing them with cords of love and bands of a man. The Lord knows that bad as men are, the key of their hearts hangs on the nail of love. He knows that His almighty goodness, though often baffled, will triumph in the end.

Grace Reveals the Evil of Sin

There is no fear that the doctrine of grace will lead men to sin, because iniquity is made to be exceedingly bitter before it is forgiven or when it is forgiven. When God begins to deal with a man, He usually causes him to see his evil ways in all their heinousness. He makes him look on sin until he cries out with David, "My sin is ever before me" (Ps. 51:3). In my own case, when I was under conviction of sin, my soul saw only darkness and a horrible tempest. It seemed as if a horrible spot were painted on my eyeballs. Guilt so drew around me that I could not rest from the anticipation of the wrath to come. I felt that I had offended God and that this was the most awful thing a human could do. Even to this hour, a sight of sin causes the most dreadful emotions in my heart like the deep horror a burned child feels toward fire. By the operations of grace, we are made weary of sin, and we loathe both it and its imaginary pleasure. We would utterly exterminate it from the soil of our nature. One of the sure fruits of the Spirit is a love of holiness and a loathing of every false way. A deep inward experience forbids the child of God to sin. He has known within himself its judgment and its condemnation, and henceforth it is a thing abhorrent to him. Hence, the fear that grace will be abused is abundantly safeguarded.

Grace Makes One a New Creature

The doctrine of grace ceases to be dangerous in the hands of one who is quickened by the Holy Spirit and created anew in the image of God. The Spirit of God has come and transformed the man, removing his ignorance, changing his affections, enlightening his understanding, subduing his will, refining his desires, changing his life. In fact, he is a newborn in the Spirit. This change is compared in Scripture to the resurrection from the dead, to a creation, and to a new birth. "Ye must be born again," said Christ to Nicodemus (John 3:7), and gracious men are born again. To the believer, the abounding grace of the Father is a bond to righteousness that the believer never thinks of breaking. Believers feel the sweet constraints of sacred gratitude and desire to perfect holiness in the fear of the Lord. All beings live according to their nature, and the regenerated man works out the holy instincts of his renewed mind. He cries after holiness, wars against sin, labors to be pure in all things, and puts forth all his strength toward that which is pure and perfect. A new heart makes all the difference. Rather than leading to sin, the blessings of almighty love suggest the loftiest of aspirations.

Cleansing Through Atonement

The blood of Jesus cleanses as well as pardons. The sinner learns that his free pardon cost the life of his best Friend, the Son of God. This causes a sacred mourning for sin as he looks upon the Lord whom he pierced. Love for Jesus burns in the pardoned sinner's breast, and therefore the pardoned sinner feels a burning indignation against the murderous evil of sin. To him all manner of evil is detestable, since it is stained with the Savior's heart's blood. The penitent sinner is horrified to hear the Son of God cry, "Eloi, sabachthani!" because of his sin. From the death of Jesus, the mind draws the conclusion that sin is exceedingly sinful in the sight of the Lord, for if eternal justice would not even spare the well-beloved Jesus when imputed sin was upon Him, how much less will it spare guilty men? It must be a thing unutterably full of poison that could make even the immaculate Jesus suffer so terribly. Nothing can be imagined that can have greater power over gracious minds than the vision of a crucified Savior denouncing sin by all His wounds and by every drop of falling blood. What? Live in the sin that slew Jesus? Find pleasure in that which brought His death? Impossible! Thus, you see, free grace when handed down by a pierced hand is never likely to suggest self-indulgence in sin, but the very reverse is true.

Daily Help from God's Spirit

God the Holy Ghost has purposed to dwell in the bosom of every man whom God has saved by His grace. Is that not a wonderful means of sanctification? By what other can men be kept from sin than by having God Himself dwell in their hearts? The ever-blessed Spirit leads believers to be much in prayer, and what a power of holiness is found in the child of grace speaking to the heavenly Father! The tempted soul flies to his God and unbosoms his grief, looking to the flowing wounds of his Redeemer, and comes down strong to resist temptation. The divine Word also, with its precepts and promises, is a never-failing source of sanctification. Were it not that we bathe every day in the sacred fountain of eternal strength, we might soon be weak and irresolute. But fellowship with God renews us in our vigorous warfare with sin. The Spirit also frequently quickens the believer's conscience so that things that did not seem sinful in the past now strike him as sinful as seen in a clearer light. The natural conscience is hard and callous, but the gracious conscience grows more and more tender till at last it becomes as sensitive as a raw wound. He who has most grace is most conscious of his need of more grace. Have you not felt this holy fear, this sacred caution? It is by this means that the Holy Spirit prevents your ever turning your liberty to licentiousness.

In addition to this, the good Spirit leads us into hallowed intercourse with God, and I defy a man to live upon the mount with God and then come down to transgress like men of the world. If you have walked the palace floor of glory and seen the King in His beauty, till the light of His countenance has been your heaven, you cannot be content with the gloom and murkiness of the tents of wickedness. To lie, to deceive, to pretend as the men of the world do, no longer lies within you. If you indeed dwell with God, the perfume of the ivory palaces will be with you, and men will know that you do not dwell with them. It is the child living with His father in a family of love. Where else could he find better to live? In a thousand ways, all danger of our presuming upon the grace of God is effectually removed.

Partakers of the Grace of God

Those who believe the doctrine of grace are lifted up above the basic concerns of the world for food and clothes. Their minds are led to consider the noble themes of everlasting covenant, predestination, immutable love, effectual calling, God in Christ, the work of the Spirit, justification, sanctification, adoption. Others play with little sand heaps on the seashore, but the believer walks in free grace among hills and mountains. The themes of thought around him tower upward, Alps on Alps. The man's mental stature rises with his surroundings, and he becomes a thoughtful being, communing with sublimities. This is the way to deliverance from vices and degrading lusts. Thoughtlessness is the prolific mother of iniquity. It is a hopeful sign when minds begin to roam among lofty truths. The man who has been taught of God to think will not so readily sin as the being whose mind is buried beneath his flesh. Now he dwells in the presence of God, and life to him is real, earnest, and sublime. He cares not to scrape together gold with the rake of the covetous, for he is immortal and must seek eternal gains. He feels that he is born for divine purposes and inquires, "Lord, what would You have me do?" He feels that as God has loved him, so God's love may flow forth to others. We are each one as a lamp kindled that we may shine in the dark and light up other lamps.

New hopes come crowding on the man who is saved by grace. His immortal spirit enjoys glimpses of the endless. As God has loved him in time, he believes that the like love will bless him in eternity. He has no fear for the future for he knows that his Redeemer lives. Even while here below, he begins to sing the songs of the angels, for his spirit spies from afar the dawn of the glory yet to be revealed. Thus, with joyous heart and light footstep he goes forward to the unknown future as merrily as to a wedding feast.

Put out the hand of faith and grasp your portion. Trust Jesus with your soul and receive your legacy.

*T*hink of it: the very Christ who died on Calvary is He by whom you will be sentenced. God will judge the world by the man Christ Jesus. He it is who will come in the clouds of heaven and gather all nations before Him, and when those who have despised Him shall look upon His face, they will be terrified beyond conception. Not the lightnings, not the thunders, not the dreadful sound of the last tremendous trump shall so alarm them as that face of injured love. Then will they cry to the mountains and hills to hide them from the face of Him who sits upon the throne (Rev. 6:16). Why, it is the face of Him who wept for sinners, the face that scoffers stained with bloody drops extracted by the thorny crown, the face of the incarnate God, who came to save mankind in infinite mercy! But because they have despised Him, preferring their own lusts to infinite love and persisting in rejecting God's best proof of kindness, the sight of that face shall be for them more accusing and condemning than all else besides. How dreadful is this truth! The more you consider it, the more it fills the soul with terror. Would to God that it might drive us to fly to Jesus, for then we will behold Him with joy in that day.

Chapter Nine

The Greatest Wonder of Grace

And I was left—Ezekiel 9:8.

SALVATION NEVER SHINES SO BRIGHTLY to any man's eyes as when it comes to himself. Then is grace illustrious indeed, when we can see it working with divine power upon ourselves. To our personal understanding, our own case is ever the most desperate, and the mercy shown to us is the most extraordinary. We see others perish and wonder that the same doom has not befallen us. The horror of the ruin that we dreaded and our intense delight at the certainty of safety in Christ unite with our personal sense of unworthiness to make us cry in amazement with Ezekiel, "And I was left."

Ezekiel saw in a vision the slaughtermen slaying those to the right and left at the bidding of divine justice, and as he stood unharmed among the heaps of the slain, he exclaimed with surprise, "I was left." It may be that the day will come when we, too, shall cry with solemn joy, "And I by sovereign grace am spared!" Special grace will cause us to marvel. Emphatically will it be so at the last dread day.

Read the story of the gross idolatry of the people of Jerusalem as recorded in the eighth chapter of Ezekiel's prophecy, and you will not wonder at the judgment with which the Lord at length overthrew the city. Let us consider how the Lord dealt with the guilty people. "Six men came . . . from the north, and every man a slaughter weapon in his hand" (Ezek. 9:2). The destruction they brought was swift and terrible, and it was typical of other solemn visitations. All through history the observing eye notices lines of justice, red marks upon the page where the Judge of all the earth has at last seen it needful to decree a terrible visitation upon a guilty people. All these past displays of divine vengeance point to a coming judgment even more complete and overwhelming. The past is prophetic of the future. A day is surely coming when the Lord Jesus, who came once to save, will descend a second time to judge. Despised mercy has always been followed by deserved wrath, and so it must be in the end of all things. "But who may abide the day of his coming? and who shall stand when he appeareth?" (Mal. 3:2). He shall lift the balances of justice and make bare the sword of execution. When His avenging angels shall gather the vintage of the earth, who among us shall exclaim in wondering gratitude, "And I was left"? Such will be a wonder of grace indeed!

I will use the wonderfully descriptive vision of this chapter that we may with holy fear behold *the character of the doom* from which grace delivers us. Then I will dwell upon the exclamation of our text, "I was left," considering it as the joyful utterance of *the persons who are privileged to escape the destruction*. And, last, I will outline *the emotions that the escaped feel*.

The Terrible Doom

In the vision where the prophet Ezekiel saw himself preserved, begin by noticing that it was a *just* punishment inflicted upon those who had been often warned. God said that if they set up idols, He would destroy them, for He would not endure such an insult to His Godhead. He had often pleaded with them through words and with severe providences, for their land had been laid desolate, their city had been besieged, and their kings had been carried away captive. But they were bent on backsliding to the worship of their idols. Therefore, when the sword of the Lord was drawn, it was not an unexpected judgment. Similarly, in the close of life and at the end of the world when judgment comes upon mankind, it will be just and according to the solemn warnings of the Word of God.

When I read the terrible things that are written in God's book in reference to future punishment, I am greatly pressed in spirit. Some sit in judgment upon the great Judge and condemn His punishment as too severe. As for me, I cannot measure the power of God's anger. Let it burn as it may, I am sure that it will be just. No needless pain will be inflicted upon a single one of God's creatures. Even those who are doomed forever will endure no more than justice absolutely requires, no more than they themselves will admit to be the due reward of their sins. This is the very hell of hell that men will know that they are justly suffering. Sin and suffering are indissolubly bound together in the constitution of nature; it cannot be otherwise, nor should it be. It is right that evil is punished. Those who were punished in Jerusalem could not turn upon the executioners and say, "We do not deserve this." Every cruel wound and every fierce crash of the Babylonian battle-ax fell on those who in their conscience knew that they were only reaping what they had themselves sown. What wonders of grace shall we be if at the last we shall be rescued from the judgment that we have so richly deserved!

Let us notice very carefully that this slaughter was *preceded by a separation* that removed those who were distinct in character from among the people. Before the judgment, a man appeared among them clothed in linen with a writer's inkhorn by his side, who marked all those who in their hearts were grieved at the evil done in the city. Until they were marked, the destroyers did not commence their work. The Lord carefully preserves His own when He lays bare His arm for war. We read in the Revelation that the angel said, "Hurt not the earth, neither the sea, nor the trees, till we have sealed the servants of our God in their foreheads" (7:3). Vengeance must sheath her sword till love has housed its darlings. Before the elements shall melt with fervent heat and the pillars of the universe shall rock and reel beneath the weight of wrathful deity, Christ shall first catch away His people so that they shall be ever with the Lord. He shall divide the nations as a shepherd divides his sheep from the goats, and no sheep of His shall be destroyed. Oh, that we may be among the selected ones and prove His power to keep us in the day of wrath. May each of us say, amid the wreck of matter and the crash of worlds, "And I was left." It will be so if you hate the sins by which you are surrounded and if you have received the mark of the blood of Jesus upon your soul. If not, you will not escape, for there is no other saving door.

Next, this judgment was placed *in the Mediator's hands*. Observe that in Ezekiel 9, there was no slaughter done except where the man with the writer's inkhorn led the way. We also read in the tenth chapter that "one cherub stretched forth his hand from between the cherubims unto the fire that was between the cherubims, and took thereof, and put it into the hands of him that was clothed with linen: who took it, and went out" (vs. 7), and cast it over the city. God's glory of old shone forth between the cherubim, over the place of propitiation and atonement, and as long as the glow of light remained, no judgment fell on Jerusalem. But later, "the glory of the LORD went up from the cherub, and stood over the threshold of the house" (vs. 4), and then judgment was near to come. When God no longer deals with men in Christ, His wrath burns like fire, and He commissions the ambassador of mercy to be the messenger of wrath. The very man who marked with his pen the saved one threw burning coals upon the city and led the way for the destruction of the sinful. What does this teach but this: "For the Father judgeth no man, but hath committed all judgment unto the Son" (John 5:22).

I know of no truth more dreadful to meditate upon. Think of it: the very Christ who died on Calvary is He by whom you will be sentenced. God will judge the world by the man Christ Jesus. He it is who will come in the clouds of heaven and gather all nations before Him, and when those who have despised Him shall look upon His face, they will be terrified beyond conception. Not the lightnings, not the thunders, not the dreadful sound of the last tremendous trump shall so alarm them as that face of injured love. Then will they cry to the mountains and hills to hide them from the face of Him who sits upon the throne (Rev. 6:16).

Why, it is the face of Him who wept for sinners, the face that scoffers stained with bloody drops extracted by the thorny crown, the face of the incarnate God, who came to save mankind in infinite mercy! But because they have despised Him, preferring their own lusts to infinite love and persisting in rejecting God's best proof of kindness, the sight of that face shall be for them more accusing and condemning than all else besides. How dreadful is this truth! The more you consider it, the more it fills the soul with terror. Would to God that it might drive us to fly to Jesus, for then we will behold Him with joy in that day.

This destruction *began at the sanctuary*. The Lord says, "Begin at my sanctuary" (Ezek. 9:6). Begin at the chief and front of the religious world; begin with the high professors who are looked up to as examples. I wonder if the Lord were to visit our city in His anger, where He would begin. I think He would begin at the churches, beginning with the preachers and teachers and bishops and church members. What does Peter say? "For the time is come that judgment must begin at the house of God: and if it first begin at us, what shall the end be of them that obey not the gospel of God? And if the righteous scarcely be saved, where shall the ungodly and the sinner appear?" (1 Pet. 4:17–18).

The first thing the slaughtermen did was to slay the ancient men who were before the temple, even the seventy elders of the people, for they were secret idolaters. You may be sure that the sword that did not spare the chief men and fathers made quick work of those of even baser heart. Those in church leadership roles must not expect to find a more lenient treatment than others at the last great judgment. Rather, if there shall be a specially careful testing on sincerity, it will be for those who have taken upon themselves to lead others to the Savior. To play the hypocrite is to play the fool. Will a man deceive his Maker or delude the Most High? It cannot be. Church members should consider this well, for judgment will begin there. When the Lord's avengers come forth, it is there the havoc will begin! How fiercely shall the sword sweep through the hosts of carnal professors, those who call themselves God's servants but who are slaves of the devil. There are those who drink of the cup of the Lord but are drunken with the wine of their own lusts, who can lie and cheat and commit fornication and yet dare approach the table of the Lord. What cutting and hewing there will be among this group. It would have been better for such people to never have been born. The word is terrible to all who have a name to live and are dead. God grant that in such testing times, when many fail, we may survive every ordeal and exclaim in the end, "And I was left."

After the executioners had begun at the sanctuary, they *did not spare any except those upon whom was the mark*. Old and young, men and women, priests and lay people, all were slain. So in the last day, all sinners who have not fled to Christ will perish. Either the mark of Christ's pen or the mark of Christ's sword must be upon everyone. There will be no sparing of one because he was rich or of another because he was educated or of another because he was eloquent or of another because he was held in high esteem. Those who are marked with the blood of Christ are safe! Do you wear it? Or will you die in your sins? Bow down before the feet of Jesus and beseech Him to mark you as His own. May you be one of those who will joyfully cry, "And I was left."

The Persons Who Escaped

Every person who escaped could say, "And I was left." We are told that those were marked for mercy who sighed and cried "for all the abominations that be done in the midst thereof" (Ezek. 9:4). Remember that this is God's Word and not mine. Hear and weigh it for yourself. We do not read that the devouring sword passed by those quiet people who never did anybody any harm. Neither does it say that the Lord saved those who were judicious and maintained a good name and repute until death. The only people who were saved were those who were exercised in heart, and that heart-work was of a painful kind. They sighed and cried because of abounding sin. They saw it, protested it, avoided it, and, last of all, wept over it continually. Where testimony failed, it remained for them to mourn. They sat down and sighed their hearts away because of the evils that they could not cure. When that sighing alone did no good, they took to crying in prayer to

God that He would come and put an end to the dreadful ills that brooded over the land.

I wonder, if I were able to read the secret lives of those professing faith, whether I would find that they sigh and cry over the sin of others. Would a tenth of them be exercised in heart? I am afraid that it does not cause some people much anxiety when they see sin rampant around them. They say that they are sorry, but it never causes them much trouble. Did you ever feel as if your heart would break over an ungodly son? Did you ever feel as if you could lay down your life to save that daughter of yours? When you have gone through the street and seen the moral filth, has not your blood chilled in you? If you can go up and down in the world fully at ease because you are prospering in life, if you forget about the surrounding sin and poverty and the yet greater woe that is coming, there cannot be much grace in you. How does the love of God dwell in you? "Are we to always be miserable?" asks one. Far from it. There are many other things that make us rejoice, but if the sad state of those around us does not cause us to sigh and cry, we have not the grace of God in us. The true believer loves his race and cannot bear to see men sinning, dishonoring God, and ruining themselves. It sometimes lies upon my heart like a huge mountain that crushes my spirit to think that Jesus should be rejected, His precious name be blasphemed, and the gospel make so little progress in our land. May God break in, even if it costs the lives of thousands of us, for we would be glad to die to save our country from so dire a curse of sin! I am happy enough when I think Christ's kingdom comes, but nothing beneath the sky can give me satisfaction if my Lord's work is at a standstill. We must be so taken up with the glory of God that the wickedness of mankind grieves us to the heart.

But those who escaped the slaughter were preserved because of the mark. We must all bear the mark of Jesus Christ. It is the mark of faith in the atoning blood. That sets apart the chosen of the Lord, and that alone. If you have that mark, in that last day no sword of justice can come near you. "Come not near any man upon whom is the mark" (Ezek. 9:6). It will not come even near the marked ones. The grace-marked soul is safe even from the near approach of ill. Let him alone, you bearers of the destroying weapons. Just as the angel of death, when he flew through the land of Egypt, was forbidden to touch a house where the blood of the lamb was on the lintel and the two side posts, so is it sure that avenging justice cannot touch the man who is in Christ Jesus. Who is he who condemns since Christ has died? If you are registered by the man clothed in linen, you will be able to say, "And I was left."

The Emotions of the Prophet

Ezekiel saw men falling right and left, and *he* himself stood like a lone rock amidst a sea of blood, and he cried in wonder, "And I was left."

But there is even more. "I fell on my face." He lay *prostrate with humility*. Have a hope that you are saved? Then fall on your face! See the hell from which you are delivered, then bow before the Lord. Why are you saved more than anyone else? Certainly not because of any merit in you. It is due to the sovereign grace of God alone.

If a man has been a drunkard and then been led to flee to Christ, when he says, "And I was left," he will feel the hot tears rising to his eyes, for many other drinkers have died in delirium. Indeed, every saved person is a marvel to himself. No one wonders more at divine grace in his salvation than me. Why was I called and saved? I cannot make it out, and I never shall. But I will always praise and bless and magnify my Lord for casting an eye of love upon me. Will you not do the same? Will you not fall on your face and bless the mercy that makes God your Father?

What did the prophet do next? Finding that he was left, he *began to pray for others*. "Ah LORD GOD!" said Ezekiel, "wilt thou destroy all the residue of Israel?" (Ezek. 9:8). Intercession is an instinct of the renewed heart. When the believer finds that he is safe, he must pray for others. Though the prophet's prayer was too late, ours need not be. We shall be heard when we pray for the perishing. Ask God, who has spared you, to spare those who are like you. Do not rest till you have wrestled with God for their salvation. Bow your head at once and cry to God for them.

May God hear that prayer if it has come from the lips of sincerity. I could not endure the thought of missing one of my boys in heaven. I am in deep sympathy with any of you who have not seen your household brought to Christ. Oh, for grace to pray earnestly and labor zealously for the salvation of our whole household!

And how about your neighbors, fellow workers, friends, and companions in business? Have you spoken with them? It is wonderful what a kind word will do. Have you tried? "But we must not be too pushy," says one. I do not know about that. If you saw people in a burning building, nobody would blame you for pushing your way in to help save them. When a man is sinking in the river, who would blame you for jumping in to pull him out? This world has been lost, and it must be saved. We must get a grip of sinking sinners somehow, even it is by the hairs of their head as they sink, for if they sink, they are lost forever. We must not permit them to die without a knowledge of the truth.

If you are left while others perish, I beseech you by the mercies of God, by the heart of compassion that is in Christ Jesus, by the bleeding wounds of the dying Son of God, love your fellow men and sigh and cry about them if you cannot bring them to Christ. If you cannot save them, you can weep over them. If you cannot give them a drop of cold water in hell, you can give them your heart's tears while yet they are in this body.

We who are constitutionally despondent must not give way to depression. We must cry to God to help us by the divine Comforter and aim at being joyful Christians. We have abundant reasons for being cheerful, for the Father Himself loves us and has given us everlasting comfort in Christ Jesus. Let us not be so unwise and ungrateful as to neglect these consolations of the Spirit. If the fountain flows so freely, why should we be thirsty? If we wear a dark countenance, we may distress the weak ones in the family of God and spread the infection of depression. Let us wear our sackcloth on our loins if we must wear it, but let us not wave it in everyone's face lest we offend the Lord's people. Is it not clear from the Word that we shall be damaged if we give way to apprehension and dismay? Is it not apparent that we are invigorated, equipped, and prepared for our Lord's service when we are strong in the Lord and in the power of His might? Therefore, let us breathe earnestly to God the desire that His everlasting consolation may enrich our spirits and that our hearts may be comforted at this moment.

Chapter Ten

Free Grace a Motive for Free Giving

Now our Lord Jesus Christ himself, and God, even our Father, which hath loved us, and hath given us everlasting consolation and good hope through grace, comfort your hearts, and stablish you in every good word and work—2 Thessalonians 2:16–17.

THE THESSALONIAN SAINTS had been persecuted and afflicted, and they had exhibited such great faith that Paul says, "So that we ourselves glory in you in the churches of God for your patience and faith" (2 Thess. 1:4). As if they did not have enough trouble coming from the outside, there sprang up in their midst certain hot-headed teachers who declared that the day of Christ was immediately at hand. The coming of the Lord is the grandest hope of the church, and it is an evidence of the extreme power of error to poison and pervert truth that our brightest consolation can be so twisted as to cause the saints to be "shaken in mind" and troubled. So it appears to be with the Thessalonians. They were perplexed with mysterious rumors that the zealots probably supported by a misinterpretation of the apostle's own language in his first letter to them. It appears that they were tempted to leave their normal lifestyle and even their business occupations because the world was so speedily coming to an end. Since this created a great deal of confusion among the church members, Paul wrote them this second letter to establish them in the truth and keep them from evil. Paul felt that it was of the utmost importance that this honorable church should be at rest and not lack consolation as to either its bitter persecutions or its internal difficulties.

The Importance of Believers Enjoying Consolation

We must never say that it does not matter whether we are doubting or believing, sighing or rejoicing. It does matter a great deal. Every commander knows that if his soldiers are not in good heart, numbers and training do not mean victory in battle. Courage is essential to valor. The Lord's word to His people has always been: "Be strong and of good courage" (Josh. 1:6). He would have those who know His glorious gospel to live a life of blessedness, that they may serve Him better. Does not His Spirit say, "Rejoice in the Lord alway: and again I say, Rejoice" (Phil. 4:4)? Has He not given the Comforter that He may continually console us? Believers bring far more glory to His name if they are filled with joy and peace in believing than if they yield to despondency. "The joy of the LORD is your strength" (Neh. 8:10).

That the Lord would have us be of good courage is *implied in the very existence of our text*. It is the prayer of an inspired man. Paul wrote under the guidance of the Holy Spirit when he penned his prayer, "Now our Lord Jesus Christ himself, and God, even our Father, . . . comfort your hearts, and stablish you in every good word and work." It is on God's record forever that all Christians should value consolation, even as it was valued by one who was a tender lover of the flock of Christ. To lightly esteem what the experienced apostle to the Gentiles valued would be a great presumption on our part.

Paul expresses this prayer in a deeply solemn form, for he writes: "Now our Lord Jesus Christ *himself*." Was there need for that word *himself*? He gives great emphasis that the Lord Jesus in His own person and by His own power should give the Thessalonians comfort. Is that not a weighty matter that leads the reverent heart of Paul thus to plead? Nor is this all, for he goes on to say, "and God, even our Father." It is as if their need for rest requires God the Father Himself to undertake the work of comforting His people. No one else could give them such comfort as they required, but God could do it.

Nor is this the only instance in the epistle where this desire is expressed with equal force: "Now the Lord of peace himself give you peace always by all means" (2 Thess. 3:16). I do not know that in one sentence there could be compressed a more intense desire that they may be at peace. "The Lord" is invoked, and He is styled "the Lord of peace," that all His divine majesty may be seen and His peacemaking power may be displayed. "The Lord of peace" is called upon to give peace by "himself," and this is asked for "always." Peace in the cool of the evening is not enough, it is needed at all times of the day, in all the days of the year, and in every period of life, in every place, and under all circumstances. This wish is expressed with great breadth of words: "give you peace always *by all means*." If it cannot be brought by one means, let it be brought by another, but somehow or other may you enjoy the peace of the Lord that the Lord alone can create. Such a prayer as this would not have been placed among the Scriptures unless it were of the utmost importance that we should enjoy peace of mind.

Paul almost hints at one reason for this strong necessity, for in one word he lets us see that it is a vital blessing because *it affects the Christian's heart*. His expression is, "Comfort your hearts." It is wonderful to have a healthy body, but what is that compared with a healthy heart? A disease of the heart is an injury to the whole man. If anything goes wrong with the fountain, the streams of life soon feel it. The entire manhood depends upon the heart, and hence the need for comfort and the value of the promise: "he shall strengthen thine heart" (Ps. 27:14). It is a disaster when the springs of action are weakened and the spirit sinks. "The spirit of a man will sustain his infirmity; but a wounded spirit who can bear?" (Prov. 18:14). When the spirit is wounded and begins to sink, the waters have come in, even into the soul. Hence our Lord said to His disciples, "Let not your heart be troubled: ye believe in God, believe also in me" (John 14:1). Faith alone upholds the heart and enables the man to bear up under pressure. A heart without comfort will grievously affect its action and mar the entire lifeforce of one's being. "Wherefore lift up the hands which hang down, and the feeble knees" (Heb. 12:12) by saying to those who are of a feeble heart, "Be strong, fear not." Ask that the heart may rejoice in God, for then the roughness of the way and the stress of the weather will be matters of small concern.

This confidence of heart prevents impatience and other evils. Possibly it was the lack of comfort that led certain of the Thessalonians to preach the immediate coming of their Lord. Perhaps their impatience excited the wish, and the wish led to the assertion. When people lose the present comfort of plain gospel doctrines, they are likely to begin speculating, especially regarding the coming of the Lord. They left the patient waiting that is our duty for a feverish prophesying that is nowhere encouraged in the Word of God. Note that the apostle said to them in chapter three, "The Lord direct your hearts into the love of God, and into the patient waiting for Christ" (vs. 5). No one waits patiently when he is low in spirit and weary in heart. When everything is tossed about, and our hope grows dim, and our fellowship is broken, and our zeal is burning low, we jump at anything that will end the struggle and enable us to avoid further effort. Laziness and despondency lead many to cry, "Why is his chariot so long in coming?" (Judg. 5:28). You think time too long and life too long, for you are not happy where your Lord has placed you, and you are eager to rush out of the field of service into the chamber of rest. This will not do.

We must receive comfort in our spirit that we may be able to patiently toil on, however long life may be or however long our Lord may delay. If not, if we grow impatient, we may resort to rash fanatical actions like the Thessalonians. Believing that the Lord was coming, they neglected their daily responsibilities and became busybodies, wandering about from house to house and living off others who did not pretend to be quite as spiritual. They were mere stargazers, looking for the Lord's advent with their mouths open and their eyes upturned, being evermore in danger of falling into a ditch. Paul commanded them to get to work and eat their own bread (2 Thess. 3:12), and if they would not the others were to stop fellowshipping with them (2 Thess. 3:14).

If you are growing impatient for the day of the Lord, I pray that comfort of heart may cool you. Go to your daily work as if Christ were not coming at all, for should He come, you will be all the more ready to meet Him for being engaged in your calling. If I knew that the Lord would come tomorrow, I would attend to my regular duties rather than leave them to stand at the window, looking for wonders. Whether the Master comes tomorrow or in a thousand years, your wisest course is to follow your calling in His fear and for His sake. We should do our work better knowing that perhaps He may come and find us at it, but we may not neglect our duty under the pretense of His appearing. Realize that unless your heart is stayed upon God, you will not go on conscientiously plodding in your duties. You will run after this novelty and that if your mind is not resting in Jesus. Thus, we see why Paul was so concerned in his prayer for the Thessalonians.

I am sure that this comfort is extremely desirable because *it promotes fruitfulness*. The apostle more than hints at this: "Comfort your hearts, and stablish you in every good word and work." When we are not happy in the Lord, we do not give ourselves heartily to His service. We grow impatient, and then we need the later exhortation: "But ye, brethren, be not weary in well doing" (2 Thess. 3:13). If we feel that Jesus is ours, that all things are working for good, and that eternal glory is ours by a sure covenant, we are moved by gratitude to a complete consecration, for the love of Christ constrains us (2 Cor. 5:14). Doubts and anxieties take us from the Master's work, but when He gives us rest, we take His yoke cheerfully and find in it yet further rest unto our souls (Matt. 11:29–30). When our hearts sing, our hands toil, and we cannot do enough for our redeeming Lord. Thus, we are established in our work, so that we delight to labor on until He shall come who shall say, "Well done, good and faithful servant ... enter thou into the joy of thy lord" (Matt. 25:23).

So it all comes to this. We who are constitutionally despondent must not give way to depression. We must cry to God to help us by the divine Comforter and aim at being joyful Christians. We have abundant reasons for being cheerful, for the Father Himself loves us and has given us everlasting comfort in Christ Jesus. Let us not be so unwise and ungrateful as to neglect these consolations of the Spirit. If the fountain flows so freely, why should we be thirsty? If we wear a dark countenance, we may distress the weak ones in the family of God and spread the infection of depression. Let us wear our sackcloth on our loins if we must wear it, but let us not wave it in everyone's face lest we offend the Lord's people. Is it not clear from the Word that we shall be damaged if we give way to apprehension and dismay? Is it not apparent that we are invigorated, equipped, and prepared for our Lord's service when we are strong in the Lord and in the power of His might? Therefore, let us breathe earnestly to God the desire that His everlasting consolation may enrich our spirits and that our hearts may be comforted at this moment.

The Gospel Comfort Is Freely Bestowed

"Now our Lord Jesus Christ himself, and God, even our Father, which hath loved us, and hath *given us* everlasting consolation." Observe that the comforts bestowed upon believers are free because *they are described as a gift*. The old proverb has it, "Nothing is freer than a gift." Every blessing that we receive from God comes as a gift. We have earned nothing, so what would we have to purchase it with? What work did we ever do that could deserve everlasting consolation from the hand of the great Lord? Comfort in Christ is an absolutely free, spontaneous gift of sovereign grace because the Lord has a right to do as He wills, but certainly on no account of anything we have done or ever shall do. If you have any comfort or triumph in God, it is God who has given you your holy joy.

The freeness of this gift is seen in every part of it. The comfort given to us from God is very complete, but it is as manifestly free as it is evidently perfect. It covers *the past* with these golden words: "which hath loved us"; as for *the present*, it is enriched with this truth: "hath given us everlasting consolation"; and as for *the future*, it is glorified with this blessing: "and good hope through grace." Here is a triple comfort of indescribable worth.

He "hath loved us." Why is this? Come, you wise men, pry into *the ancient past* and tell me why God loved His chosen. Stand and gaze as long as you will into the eternal mind, but the only reply out of the excellent glory falls from Jesus' lips: "Even so, Father: for so it seemed good in thy sight" (Matt. 11:26). Shall not the King of kings dispense His favors as He wills? He has loved us "before the foundation of the world" (Eph. 1:4); a love so ancient cannot have been born of any human cause. Eternal love is a flame enfolding itself; it borrows no fuel from without but lives upon itself. He says, "I have loved thee with an everlasting love: therefore with lovingkindness have I drawn thee" (Jer. 31:3). But why that everlasting love, we cannot tell. By divine love, the mysterious past is made to glow with the glory of God, and its light is like a stone most precious, even like a jasper stone, clear as crystal. Once when we looked back into the past, we saw the blackness of our guilt and the hole of the pit we were taken from, but now we behold a silver stream of mercy flowing from the throne of God and of the Lamb, and we track it to the eternal purpose of love and the covenant of grace. Gaze as you can into light ineffable, but even with the eye of faith, all that you can discern in the ages that are past is the splendor beyond compare of the word *LOVE*. In eternity the Lord loved us. How free this is! How much we owe for it! The past is bright with love, with love most free.

As for *the present*, "he hath given us everlasting consolation." We have it now. The pardon of sin is ours, the perfect righteousness of Christ is ours, life in Christ is ours, union with Christ is ours, marriage to Christ is ours. Glory with Christ shall be ours, but even now we have the down payment of it in the Spirit who dwells in us and shall be with us forever. All this is assuredly a gift. How could it be otherwise? Bless, then, the Giver. This would never have been ours if free grace and dying love had not brought it to us.

As for *the future*, what of that? Dark lower the clouds, and the tempest mutters from afar, and we tremble lest in the end of life, when our physical force decays, we may be overtaken with a storm of death. But this covers all: we have "good hope through grace." The Scriptures assure us that the great Shepherd will be with us in the valley of death-shade and that after death there is a resurrection and that with our risen body we shall behold the King in His beauty when He shall stand in the latter days upon the earth. This is so good a hope that it fills all the future with music. This, too, is a gift. There is not a trace of legal claim in it; it comes not by way of reward but of divine favor. Free grace reigns through the past, in the present, and into the future.

Lest we should make any mistake, the apostle mentions *"our Lord Jesus Christ himself"* as the One from whose hand these consolations have come so freely. What a charming thought that Jesus Christ should comfort me! When the Lord sets Himself down to console His brethren, I warrant you it is done in a heavenly style. He will not fail or be discouraged. He will wash our feet if we have grown weary. He will give His bosom for a pillow to our head if the pain is there. He will anoint our eyes with salve if our eyes are failing and bind up the broken heart if that is bleeding. Lest we fall, He will put underneath us the everlasting arms, and lest we be wounded, He will spread over us the shadow of His wings. His whole being in its grandeur and His humanity in its tenderness He has given to us. He lays Himself out for us and will not leave us comfortless. He will come to us as the sympathizer in all grief and a mighty helper in all distress. What a grace is ours! Is He not full of grace and truth? "For God sent not his Son into the world to condemn the world; but that the world through him might be saved" (John 3:17). There will come a judgment day, but now the Son of God sits upon a throne of grace, and His scepter is that of love. We know that the comforts of the gospel must be graciously free, since they are brought to us by Jesus Christ Himself.

Then the apostle solemnly adds, *"and God our Father."* There seems to be a particular twist of sweetness about this. It is not "God the Father" but "God *our* Father." We love God the Father, but as "our Father," He comes nearer to us and gladdens our hearts. Now a father does not pay wages to his children; his gifts of his fatherly heart are freely bestowed on them. Thus, we see that the everlasting consolations of the gospel come freely as spontaneous donations of our great Father, whose delight it is to give good gifts to them who ask Him.

Cannot you look up at this moment and cry, "Our Father"? How sweet to feel the Spirit's witness in your soul and to cry, "Abba, Father!" The spirit of adoption is never a spirit of bondage or legality. It never boasts of human merit, but its one song is "free grace and dying love." May our Father's free favor make your heart to sing.

Look at the text again, and you will see how explicit Paul is upon one point. To make us see the freeness of those consolations that come to God's troubled people, he writes: "Our Lord Jesus Christ himself, and God, even our Father, *which hath loved us.*" Divine love is so great a truth that it is not so much a truth to speak upon with tongue as it is to enjoy in silence in the heart. I can fully understand that God pities me in my misery, but I am filled with sacred amazement when I am told that He *loves* me! Loves me! What can there be in me for the Holy Ghost to love? Why should Jesus Christ set His heart on you? Does the potter fall in love with his own clay? Wonder of wonders that the Lord should love us poor nobodies, defiled with sin, with such evil tempers and such estranged natures. That He should so love us as to actually have died for us outmiracles all the miracles of His power. Yes, His love is the source and fountain of all our mercies. There can be no question that this is free, for love is unpurchasable. Love goes not in the market, it knows nothing of price or barter. Love must go forth unbribed, unhired, or not at all, in any case. Price and purchase for divine love? Wherein would such an insinuation fall short of blackest blasphemy?

Yet, observe that because the apostle feared that we should get away from this doctrine of grace, he added, "He hath given us everlasting consolation and good hope *through grace.*" Some people do not like the sound of the word *grace.* It is too Calvinistic. I do not care what you call it, but it is the very best word in the Bible next to the name of God our Savior. It is from the grace of God that all our hope begins. Grace must reign, or man must die. All other roads are broken up; grace alone bridges the chasm to man and makes a way for traffic between heaven and earth. Grace reigns in our spiritual comfort, and grace alone. Let us glorify God for it. All the good works that adorn the Christian character are the result of God's grace and not the cause of it. Grace is given us so that we may serve God, not because we do serve God. To makes us holy is the object of divine grace, but grace did not wait until it found us holy.

This is why the consolations that God gives are "everlasting." If grace were built upon our merits, it would stand upon the foundation of mist or rest upon a shadow buttressed by a dream. But if God loved us out of pure grace, and if Jesus Christ has given us consolation out of pure love, and if our whole comfort rests upon the sovereign grace of God in Christ Jesus, there is no reason why it should ever pass away unless God's grace can evaporate. Never take confidence from your lofty feelings and your holy works or your belief that sin is dead in you. He who lies humbly at God's feet, conscious of His sin and mourning over it and resting for everything upon sovereign grace and free mercy in Christ Jesus, may keep where he is with safety, for his hope shall never fail.

Where This Leads Us

Christians should take a hearty interest in every benevolent enterprise. "Comfort your hearts, and stablish you in *every* good word and work." As a follower of Christ, everything that can do good to others is a matter in which I delight to take my share. The concerns of men concern me.

This should be done in direct actions as well as in words. "In every good word and *work.*" Some believers think that word should be everything and work nothing, but the Scriptures are not of their mind. These people speak a great deal about what they will do and talk a great deal about what others ought to do and a great deal more about what others fail to do. They go on with word, word, word, and nothing else but word. They never get as far as "work," but the apostle was careful to yoke together word and work. Direct practical assistance should be given, since our Lord loves not in word only but in deed and truth as well.

This should be done without pressure. As God has loved us spontaneously, we should do everything freely out of an overflowing heart. Give because you are delighted to give liberally, not because you feel obliged to do so. How can a gracious heart better please itself than by doing good? Give as you give to a king, for we would give the best we have if we give him anything. Let it be so in all the services you render to God. Let Him have your best, your noblest, your dearest possessions. May those who believe in the free grace of God be at the forefront of the race to serve others.

Give freely, for you have received freely.

The grace of God shall make men speak that holy and pure language that is the mark of a child of God. When the grace of God meets a person, friends know it through the person's conversation. The man who could not speak without swearing can no longer swear. The proud tongue will speak so humbly and so gently that others will hardly know the person. The one whose language was suggestive and lascivious desires to not even hear of such things much less to mention them, for it is a shame for a Christian to speak of those things. The grace of God soon rinses out a person's mouth. His wife knows it, his children know it, his co-workers know it, and some will think him a fool to speak in the manner he now does. Something so changes about his conversation that men say, "This fellow was also with Jesus of Nazareth."

Chapter Eleven

The Fruits of Grace

*In that day shall five cities in the land of Egypt speak the lan-
guage of Canaan, and swear to the LORD of hosts; one shall be
called, The city of destruction. In that day shall there be an altar
to the LORD in the midst of the land of Egypt, and a pillar at the
border thereof to the LORD. . . . And the LORD shall be known
to Egypt, and the Egyptians shall know the LORD that day. . . .
Whom the LORD of hosts shall bless, saying, Blessed be Egypt
my people, and Assyria the work of my hands, and Israel mine
inheritance*—Isaiah 19:18–25.

THIS IS A REMARKABLE PROPHECY. At-
tempts have been made to explain it, as if it were already fulfilled.
I believe all such attempts to be utter failures. The promise stands
on record to be fulfilled at some future day. In those bright days
for which some of us are looking, when the knowledge of the
Lord shall cover the earth, then shall this word to Egypt be ver-
ified, and God shall be glorified both by Egypt and by Assyria as
well as by the land of Israel.

It is most encouraging to find Egypt mentioned. You find in
Psalm 68, "Princes shall come out of Egypt; Ethiopia shall soon
stretch out her hands unto God" (vs. 31). Now this I believe is

the literal meaning of the passage. You must understand that the prophecy was give to the people of Israel, and it was given to them, as it were, to children who were using types and figures. It speaks in their language. Hence, it speaks of altars and pillars and oblations, all of which are to be understood now in the spiritual sense. The church of God has come to maturity, in which she no longer needs material altars and oblations, seeing that she has Christ to be her only altar, her only priest, and prayer and praise to be the spiritual oblation that she shall bring. I understand the prophecy to be, in brief, just this. In the latter day, Egypt will be converted as well as Assyria, and wonders of grace will be performed in that land, and the people of that land shall worship the Most High with delight.

Having said this, I am now going to use the text as *a wonderful display of the grace of God* in this promise to Egypt. I see the very heart of God revealed. I see a display of what God will do, not to Egypt only, but to others also.

God's Grace Often Comes to the Very Worst of Men

This promise comes to Egypt, the nation that was an enemy of God's people. It was over Egypt that He triumphed at the Red Sea, when Pharoah said, "Who is the Lord?" (Exod. 5:2). We regard Egypt as always being typical of the enemies of God. Yet the grace of God comes to Egypt. And so it often comes to the worst enemies that God has. Saul of Tarsus, foaming at the mouth with rage against the Christ of God, was met and conquered by eternal love, renewing his heart and making him into an apostle of Christ. And oftentimes since then, electing love has chosen those who were the most furious against Christ, and the power of the Holy Spirit has come upon them, turning the lions into lambs and making them lie down at the feet of the Savior.

The Egyptians were an utterly debased people as to their idolatry and politically as well, yet the grace of God is promised as coming to them. Oh, how wondrous is the sovereignty of God! The devil cannot dye a soul so scarlet in sin but what the blood of Christ can make it white as snow. Satan cannot drive a chosen sheep of Christ so far on the mountains of vanity or into the deserts of sin but what the great Shepherd can find that sheep and bring it back again. There is hope for the most sunken. The infinite compassion of God can reach them, and the eternal power of God can lift them up.

But there is particular emphasis in the text that one of the cities in that land of Egypt that was saved was called the City of Destruction. It had come to be named by that name, and yet God looked upon it with mercy. It seems to me that the Lord is often pleased to find the most notorious sinners and make them new men in Christ Jesus. I have some in mind now who have been to me a source of unutterable joy, yet whose characters were known and certainly not admired. They were the dread of all with whom they dwelt. I remember one whose fist had laid low many adversaries and whose vile life made the village tremble when he was filled with drink. But what a humble child he became when at last the gospel brought him down! The gospel has found some of its brightest jewels in the lowest haunts of vice. Bear the gospel into the caves of darkness, where blackness seems to be palpable and to hang like the glooms of death. Carry the everlasting torch that the divine Lord Himself has kindled, and you shall discover by its light some precious redeemed ones who will be to the praise of the glory of His grace.

This should be a very great encouragement to every person, for where there is mercy proclaimed to the chief of sinners, there is encouragement to every form of sinner to come humbly to the heavenly Father. Plead the precious blood of Jesus and obtain life and peace.

God's Grace Sends a Savior

"For they shall cry unto the LORD because of the oppressors, and he shall send them a savior, and a great one, and he shall deliver them" (Isa. 19:20). Note that Ezekiel adds the phrase, "a great one." He who comes to save is Jesus, the Son of God. He comes to save us from every stain of sin, from our propensity to sin, from the power of our habits, and from the snares of Satan.

He has come to save us from the death eternal and wrath to come. Oh, what a great Savior! A little Savior would not have answered my need, for great sin required a great atonement, and my hard heart required great grace to soften it.

Jesus Christ is great in His nature, for as God He is infinite and omnipotent. He is also great in what He has done. Look to Him on the cross. It is the Son of God pouring out His life for sinners that they may live through His death. There must be great merit in such a sacrifice. Being very God of very God, though certainly man, there can be no limit set to the value of the atonement that He made. And now that He has risen from the dead, He stands before God to plead for us, and it is no little plea—no plea that might be put back or put off. With authority He pleads before His Father's throne and points to His own wounds, and the Father's heart always yields to the Son's intercession. You have a great Savior, for He is a great pleader. And, besides that, all power is in His hands. The keys of death and hell are at his side, and the government shall be upon His shoulders, and His name shall be called Wonderful, Counsellor, the Mighty God. What a Savior we have! Dare we doubt Him? When we cast ourselves upon Him, is there not an end to all our fears, for Jesus is mighty to save.

What a powerful phrase is added: "and *he shall deliver them*"! God did not send Christ haphazardly. He did not come to save those who might perchance be saved, but He came with His eye of everlasting love fixed on those for whom the precious drops were shed. He will have these by the power of His arm, plucking them from the jaws of the lion, because with the blood of His heart He has redeemed them. May the Spirit of God lay that word *deliver* home to your heart. He shall deliver from all temptation, from all trial, from all affliction, from death itself.

Grace Transforms

The eighteenth verse said, "In that day shall five cities in the land of Egypt speak the language of Canaan." The spiritual meaning is that the grace of God shall make men speak that holy and pure language that is the mark of a child of God. When the grace of God meets a person, friends know it through the person's conversation. The man who could not speak without swearing can no longer swear. The proud tongue will speak so humbly and so gently that others will hardly know the person. The one whose language was suggestive and lascivious desires to not even hear of such things much less to mention them, for it is a shame for a Christian to speak of those things. The grace of God soon rinses out a person's mouth. His wife knows it, his children know it, his co-workers know it, and some will think him a fool to speak in the manner he now does. Something so changes about his conversation that men say, "This fellow was also with Jesus of Nazareth. . . . for thy speech bewrayeth thee" (Matt. 26:71, 73). Would it not be a mercy if God would change the speech of some in London! Even our boys in the streets sometimes talk in a way that is enough to make your blood chill. O sovereign grace, come and visit these, and change their language of Belial and Babylon to the language of Canaan, for God shall give them a pure language.

Grace Sets Men on Holy Service

"There shall be an altar to the LORD in the midst of the land of Egypt, and a pillar at the border thereof to the LORD." The sinner worships himself or serves his pleasure and Satan. When the grace of God comes, the man begins at once to serve God and become God's servant. I look around and see families that worship together where you would not have thought such a thing possible before. I see others giving of their finances to God who scorned the idea but a few years ago. Others are teaching in Sunday school who would have laughed at such a proposal only a short time ago. When the Lord gets men's hearts, He takes them into His service and makes those who were most ready to serve Satan become most willing to serve Christ.

Let us pray for the grace of God that our whole life may be a life of consecration to the living God. Oh, that our ordinary dress might be as priestly vestments, and our ordinary meals as sacraments, and ourselves as priests to the living God! May our whole life be a psalm and our whole being a hallelujah to the Most High! Where the grace of God comes with power, it makes the worst of men become the best and truest servants of the living God. Harken to the song of heaven! "Unto him that loved us, and washed us from our sins in his own blood, and hath made us kings and priests unto God and his Father; to him be glory and dominion for ever and ever" (Rev. 1:5–6).

Grace Teaches Men to Pray

We read in the twentieth verse: "They shall cry unto the LORD because of the oppressors." This is a kind of prayer that only God can teach us. You can easily read a prayer from a book, but a prayer that can be called a cry is the fruit of grace. The cry is the natural expression of distress. There is no hypocrisy in a cry. God always teaches His children to pray such prayers as those. And how sweetly do saved souls pray! Next to the song of angels, I think the prayers of new converts are among the sweetest things that ever reach our ears. When we have been believers for a long time, we are apt to get into a stilted mode of talking to God in prayer, and some men who have more gifts than graces will spend the time in words, words, words. But how has my heart leaped when I have heard a cry such as "God, be merciful to me, a sinner!" from some soul who was ready to burst with fear of the wrath to come. What a joy to hear some heart that has just found Jesus and is praising and magnifying the exceeding mercy that has put away his sin! All the clergy and ministry in the land could not teach a sinner to pray one sincere prayer, but Christ can. Wonders of grace belong to God the Holy Ghost. He that teaches us to pray will teach us to praise Him in heaven. The soul that lisps out its desires sincerely to God shall one day sing with cherubim and seraphim before the eternal throne.

Grace Instructs Men

We learn this from verse twenty-one: "And the LORD shall be known to Egypt, and the Egyptians shall know the LORD in that day." To be ignorant of the things of God is a very serious evil. But it is delightful to observe how sweetly the Holy Spirit can teach. There is no teacher like the Holy Spirit! When He transforms a sinner by grace, He can so make Jesus real that the Bible is not difficult to understand. In a short time, I have seen many lay hold upon Scripture with delight and become well instructed in the kingdom of God. "And all thy children shall be taught of the LORD" (Isa. 54:13), and when the Spirit teaches, they are taught indeed. When grace comes to a man, he must know the Father, for he has become a child. He must know the Son, for He is his only confidence. He must know the Spirit, for it is the Spirit that lives in him and has renewed him. Man can teach only your ears, but God can teach your heart. Man can write the copy only in a book, but God can write it on the fleshy tablets of your soul. The Lord can graciously instruct you in the divine teaching that will end in your being complete in Christ and your entering into His glory.

Grace Makes Even Trouble a Blessing

Read the twenty-second verse: "And the LORD shall smite Egypt: he shall smite and heal it: and they shall return even to the LORD, and he shall be entreated of them, and shall heal them." When an ungodly man is in trouble, the man has nothing whatever to sustain him, and no good comes out of the trouble. But get the heart renewed through receiving the Savior and perhaps the greatest mercies he has are those that are blessings in disguise. I heard the story of a very wealthy merchant who in his old age lost everything through a foolish speculation and came to such poverty that he determined to commit suicide. But before he could end his life, he was moved by curiosity to listen to the preaching of the gospel through a street worker, and he found the Lord. He said that in his riches he had despised the gospel, but now, when brought to the lowest, Christ had found him and given him more happiness with His cross than he had had with his wealth. Oh, to get the grace of God in your heart, and then broken limbs will be a blessing. The economic depression that brought you low will appear a very different thing now. Perhaps your lot is very lowly and your toils severe, but God's grace will gild all those dark things in such a way that you shall even learn to glory in tribulation. The Lord may "smite," but He did not leave you a stranger to Him. He made you His child whom He disciplines. What a blessing it is to have the grace of God, seeing it turn adverse circumstances into true prosperity and make our losses to be our lasting gains.

Grace Changes Our Relationships

Now to the twenty-third verse: "In that day shall there be a highway out of Egypt to Assyria, and the Assyrian shall come into Egypt, and the Egyptian into Assyria, and the Egyptians shall serve with the Assyrians." Realize that the Assyrians and Egyptians were always enemies. Century after century the feud and wars were carried on between them. But when the grace of God visits them, there shall be no more fighting. Instead the Egyptian shall go and visit the Assyrian, and the Assyrian shall visit the Egyptian. Have you never seen this happen? Two brothers are at enmity and will not speak with each other. Grace comes to them, and they immediately go to each other to be reconciled.

The gospel can break down barriers. I wouldn't give a penny for your religion if you are at enmity with anyone. How can you expect mercy in that day when you will appear before God. Genuine grace makes us forgive as we have been forgiven, and it establishes relations between those who had long been enemies to one another. A common Savior binds us together in divine love and life. You cannot help loving each other. Oh, that God would put an end in the world to all wars between nations, as well as all strifes between individuals. The gospel can so change nations and individuals by the wonders of grace that those who hated now love and enemies become friends.

Grace Blesses Men and Makes Them a Blessing

You find this affirmed in verses 24 and 25: "In that day shall Israel be the third with Egypt and with Assyria, even a blessing in the midst of the land: Whom the LORD of hosts shall bless, saying, Blessed be Egypt my people . . ." The man who was accursed before and a curse becomes blessed and a blessing. It has delighted me to find members of my church trying to do good, some in one way and some in another. But if no one knows of it but you and God, go on, go on.

It is God's work to save souls, and you are workers together with Him. If you have anything to say of the remedy that wisdom has prepared for the remedy of sin's disease, there are millions who need it. If they won't come to hear the gospel, take it to their homes. If they reject the Savior, let it not be for lack of your hunting after them. Push it in their way. In season and out of season, teach the Word. You never know where or when God will bless you. But never be discouraged because of the badness or evil of the people you try to bless. If Egypt can be saved, have faith for this Egypt. If Assyria shall be saved, have confidence in God for those who are often the worst of heathens. You shall have your reward in that day when He of the pierced hand shall distribute crowns to those who faithfully serve Him. Rewards of grace shall be given to the most obscure and unknown believers, who for His sake have sought to teach little children or reclaim the adult who has fallen into sin. Take courage—your work of faith and labor of love are not in vain in the Lord and will do wonders yet to the praise of His grace.

Him that cometh to me." There is the point. We must come to Jesus as crucified and bearing our sin. We must come to Christ as pleading before the throne and see the acceptance of our prayers there. It is not in any religious ceremony or ritual. Take heed that you do not come elsewhere, for if you rest short of anything but Christ, you rest short of the promise. But if you build on nothing less than Jesus' blood and righteousness, if you look out of self entirely to Him, then rest assured that there is no other qualification to your coming. Some come to Christ quickly, others take time for their faith to grow. Some come running, some come walking, some come crawling, and others must be carried, but so long as they come, Jesus does not cast them out. One comes with long prayers, another with but two words; one comes with tears, another without; one groans while another cannot; one has intense conviction, another does not; one is shaken over hell's fire, another is attracted to the beauties of the Savior; one must be thundered at from the top of Sinai, but another beckoned to from Calvary. Do not split upon the rock of questioning what your experience is or raising the point of how you came and when you came. The only thing of real importance is that you came to Christ.

Chapter Twelve

The Certainty and Freeness of Divine Grace

All that the Father giveth me shall come to me; and him that cometh to me I will in no wise cast out—John 6:37.

LET IT BE ALWAYS REMEMBERED that the words of Jesus Christ are full of truth and grace and that in each of these two sentences there is the surest truth and the freest grace. There will be some who will perceive the truth of the first sentence and prize it most. They read the words, "All that the Father giveth me shall come to me," and they say, "Yes. Here is a high doctrine. Here is the security of the covenant, the purpose of God effectually carried out. Here is the truth that we love and the grace in which we glory." Others overlook the first sentence lest it raise questions too hard to be answered and grasp the second sentence, "Him that cometh to me I will in no wise cast out." They say, "This is it. Here is universality of description. Here is freeness of invitation. Here is a gracious overflow of liberality. This is the gospel indeed." Proclaiming the second sentence, they neglect the first.

But let us not set one Scripture over against another or attempt to divide the living child of revelation. It is *one* and is alike glorious in all its parts. You who love to hear the gospel preached to sinners, do not be afraid of the doctrines of sovereign grace. You who love sovereign grace, do not be afraid of the free invitations of the gospel and the wide door that Jesus opens for needy sinners in many passages of Scripture. Let us receive all truth and be willing to learn every lesson that the Lord has written. We must remember that if we cannot as yet reconcile truths and know everything, we are still mortals. Some things must be unknown to us. Let us know our ignorance and despair of becoming infallible, and we shall be in the path of true wisdom.

Grace Triumphant in Speciality

We begin by observing the meaning of this passage: "All that the Father giveth me shall come to me." You perceive that *the Lord Jesus leads us up to the original position of all things.* Since a people were given to Him by the Father, it is clear that they must first have been in the Father's hand. All men are naturally in the hand of the Father from the beginning. The Father has fashioned them all and made them for His pleasure. God absolutely created all things, and His kingdom rules over all. Having a right to make laws, to issue rewards, or to threaten with punishments at His own pleasure, Jehovah sits upon the throne and judges rightly. The elect were specially in the hand of the Father, for He had chosen them. The choice is ever described as being with the Father: "I thank thee, O Father, Lord of heaven and earth, that thou hast hid these things from the wise and prudent, and hast revealed them unto babes: even so, Father; for so it seemed good in thy sight" (Luke 10:21). They belong to the Father, then, as Creator, as Governor, and as the source and fountain of election.

How often do believers forget the part that the Father has in their salvation? He is the basis and prompter of it all. Remember that He who first of all chose you was none other than our Father who is in heaven. Though our Lord Jesus Christ undertook our cause, yet it was because the Father first of all, out of His great love, gave us to the Son. Forget not the Father's grace and never cease to sing of His love.

The Savior then *proceeds to inform us of a great transaction.* He says that the Father gave His people to the Son and put them into the hands of Christ. As Jesus is God, the elect always were His own, but as the Mediator, He received them from the hand of the Father. Here was the Father's condescension in noticing us at all and in bestowing us to the Son. And here was the Son's infinite mercy and compassion in accepting such poor souls as we are at the Father's hand and counting us to be His precious jewels.

But who are these "all" of the text? Two verses later we have this explanation: "And this is the Father's will which hath sent me, that of all which he hath given me I should lose nothing, but should raise it up again at the last day" (John 6:39). The given ones are by appointment delivered from being lost and appointed to a glorious resurrection, which is not true of any but the chosen. In John 10:27–29 we find the same explanation: "My sheep hear my voice, and I know them, and they follow me: and I give unto them eternal life; and they shall never perish, neither shall any man pluck them out of my hand. My Father, which gave them me, is greater than all; and no man is able to pluck them out of my Father's hand." And if this was not explained sufficiently, we have in Jesus' prayer in John 17:6 these words: "I have manifested thy name unto the men which thou gavest me out of the world: thine they were, and thou gavest them me; and they have kept thy word."

So you see that the persons given were sheep who were brought to know the voice of the Good Shepherd and to follow Him. They are in His hand, and there they are safely kept beyond all fear of harm. Jesus manifests the Father's name unto them, and they learn to keep the Father's word. We see that there was a certain period when the eternal God gave into the hands of the Mediator a multitude that no man can number, whom He had chosen from among men to be His choice and peculiar treasure. The text speaks in the *present* tense, but other verses speak in the *past* tense. Therefore, understand that the gift of the elect to Christ was performed in the past. Before the skies were stretched abroad or the mountains lifted their heads to the clouds, God had given a people to Christ. But the deed may well be said to be performed in the present, since Christ does receive from His Father's hand

His people in *time* as well as in eternity. We are by the words of our text admitted into one of the secrets of the divine council chamber, and we rejoice as we perceive that the chosen ones belonging to the Father were transferred by Him into the hands of the Mediator.

Jesus also assures us that *this transaction in eternity involves a certain change in time.* "All that the Father giveth me shall come to me." They may be living in sin for twenty, thirty, forty, fifty, sixty, seventy years, but before their time comes to die, they shall be brought to Christ. To come to Christ signifies to turn from sin and trust Christ. Coming to Christ is a leaving of all false confidences, a renouncing of all love of sin, and a looking to Jesus as the solitary pillar of our confidence and hope. This is the sign by which the secretly chosen are made known by their openly choosing Christ because the Father has secretly chosen them. You can never know your election by any other means. If you humbly and hopefully come to Jesus and make Him all your salvation, let no doctrine of election alarm or keep you back. You are one of His, for this is the seal that He sets upon His sheep. And in due time they hear His voice, are led by Him into the green pastures of grace, follow Him through life, and are brought by Him at last to the hilltops of glory.

Observe closely that Jesus hints at *a power possessed by Him to constrain the wanderers to return.* "All that the Father giveth me *shall* come to me." There is power and majesty resting on the words *shall come.* There is no "if," "but," or "maybe," but they shall come. It is put down as an unconditional and absolute purpose of God and will of Christ that all whom the Father gave to Him shall come. "So," you ask, "Christ forces men to be saved?" I answer no, in the sense that no man was ever dragged by the hair of his head to heaven. But the Lord Jesus does, by His messengers, His Word, and His Spirit, sweetly and graciously compel men to come in that they may eat of His marriage supper. And He does not violate the free will or free agency of man. God treats men as men, and when He binds them with cords, they are cords of love. I may exercise power over another's will, and yet that other man's will may be perfectly free If I show a man that certain actions are very much to his advantage, he feels bound to follow them but is still free in so doing.

Divine grace does not do that which is inconsistent with human freedom or human nature. It means that Jesus knows how to subdue the whole man by irresistible arguments addressed to the understanding, by mighty reasons appealing to the affections, and by the mysterious influence of His Holy Spirit operating upon all the powers and passions of the soul. "(For the weapons of our warfare are not carnal, but mighty through God to the pulling down of strong holds;) casting down imaginations, and every high thing that exalteth itself against the knowledge of God" (2 Cor. 10:4–5). They are the invincible artillery of the love of Christ and the sword of the Spirit which is the Word of God.

There is an influence put forth by the Holy Spirit that makes men willing in the day of God's power. Let the devil do his worst, and let the human will do its utmost, and let temptations strain themselves to the last degree of intensity, yet every soul that is numbered in the covenant of grace *shall* be brought to the foot of the cross and cry, "What must I do to be saved?"

Concluding our remarks on this first sentence, *the Savior declares that there is no exception to this rule of grace.* He says, "*All* that the Father giveth me shall come to me." Not *some* of them, but *all*. It will be found when the archangel's trumpet shall ring through earth and heaven that every soul whom God ordained to eternal life has attained that eternal life to His praise and honor. Such is the greatest comfort to those who preach the Word. Day after day we proclaim our Master's truth, and yet to a great extent we have to cry with Isaiah: "Who hath believed our report? and to whom is the arm of the Lord revealed?" (Isa. 53:1). So many resist and turn a deaf ear to the warnings of the gospel. Have we labored in vain? No, not in any way. The purpose of God is certainly fulfilled in every jot and tittle, and the Master's will is definitely and in every point accomplished. Therefore, we labor with no broken heart and preach with no coward spirit in this matter. The great plans of sovereign mercy shall not be thwarted by the enmity of man. Jehovah shall yet in the end get the victory. Some may reject the Master's invitation, but there are myriads who shall be washed in the blood of Christ and shall rejoice in its power to cleanse.

If we understand this first sentence of our text, it involves *the doctrine of election*—there are some whom the Father gave to Christ. It involves *the doctrine of effectual calling*—these who are given must and shall come. And it also teaches *the indispensable necessity of faith*, for even those who are given to Christ are not saved except they come to Christ. There is no other door to heaven but Jesus Christ. I must not expect that I shall be saved by my morality, integrity, or generosity. It is the indispensible requisite for princes and peasants, for sages and savages, for the polite and the uneducated, for the most virtuous and the most vile to come, just as they are, and accept the mercy of God freely presented to them in the person of Christ Jesus. It is this mark that the chosen of God are known.

Grace Triumphant in Its Liberality

We move on to explore the meaning of the second sentence: "Him that cometh to me I will in no wise cast out."

Please observe the liberality of *the character*: it is *"him that cometh."* It means the rich, the poor, the great, the obscure, the moral, the debased who have sunken into the worst of crimes, those who have mounted to the best of virtues, and those who are akin to devils. Any him that comes to Christ shall not be cast out. To *come* is *to leave* something and *to go to* something else. We leave every other ground of trust and make Christ our solitary hope. We come to His blood to be washed, to His righteousness to be cleansed, to His wounds to be healed, to His life for life eternal, and to His death for the death of our sins. He who thinks himself to have gone furthest into sin may yet see that this text provides a door wide open of mercy that shuts out no comer.

John Newton was a blasphemer of so gross a kind that even the sailors on the ship in a storm said that they should never get to port with such a sinner as Newton on board. But he came to Christ and was not cast out but lived to preach the Word. John Bunyan was so foul that even a wicked woman of the street who passed by him was heard to say that he was enough to corrupt the whole parish. Bunyan came to Christ and was not cast out but lived to have the honor of suffering for his Master and to win multitudes of souls to Christ. Saul of Tarsus had stained himself with the blood of saints and was a terror to the church, yet when he fell on his face and cried for mercy, he was not cast out. Any kind of *him*—no matter how evil or how good—who comes to Christ shall not be cast out. The point is whether you will come.

The next point of liberality is in the *coming*. "Him that cometh *to me*." There is the point. We must come to Jesus as crucified and bearing our sin. We must come to Christ as pleading before the throne and see the acceptance of our prayers there. It is not in any religious ceremony or ritual. Take heed that you do not come elsewhere, for if you rest short of anything but Christ, you rest short of the promise. But if you build on nothing less than Jesus' blood and righteousness, if you look out of self entirely to Him, then rest assured that there is no other qualification to your coming. Some come to Christ quickly, others take time for their faith to grow. Some come running, some come walking, some come crawling, and others must be carried, but so long as they come, Jesus does not cast them out. One comes with long prayers, another with but two words; one comes with tears, another without; one groans while another cannot; one has intense conviction, another does not; one is shaken over hell's fire, another is attracted to the beauties of the Savior; one must be thundered at from the top of Sinai, but another beckoned to from Calvary. Do not split upon the rock of questioning what your experience is or raising the point of how you came and when you came. The only thing of real importance is *that you came* to Christ.

Observe the liberality of *the time*. "Him that cometh." It does not say *when*. We may be seven or seventy when we come. Your candle may be little more than a snuff, but He will not quench it. And time does not deplete the supply of Christ's mercy. Nearly two thousand years have been spent, and there is nothing old or decrepid about Christ's love. It is never too late. God waits to be gracious and stands with outstretched arms. If you will come, He will not cast you out.

Further notice that there is no limit to *the duration* of the promise. The original reads: "I will not, not cast thee out," or "I will never, never cast thee out." This is a mercy that extends forever. Suppose the believer sins after coming? "If any man sin, we have an advocate with the Father, Jesus Christ the righteous" (1 John 2:1). Suppose that believers backslide? "I will heal their backsliding, I will love them freely: for mine anger is turned away from him" (Hos. 14:4). But believers may fall under temptation? "God is faithful, who will not suffer you to be tempted above that ye are able; but will with the temptation also make a way to escape, that ye may be able to bear it" (1 Cor. 10:13). But the believer may fall into sin as David did? Yes, but He will "purge me with hyssop, and I shall be clean: wash me, and I shall be whiter than snow" (Ps. 51:7). Christ will never suffer one who has once been grasped in His hands to be taken away. "I give unto them eternal life; and they shall never perish, neither shall any man pluck them out of my hand" (John 10:28). Is this not a precious mercy. We shall abide forever! Ours is no longer receiving the spirit of bondage again to fear, but receiving the spirit of adoption where we cry, "Abba, Father!"

Still we have not exhausted the text. Something of liberality of this passage is to be found in *its certainty*. "I will *in no wise* cast out." It is *a certainty* that Christ will accept you. If there were only half a shadow of a hope that Jesus Christ would have mercy upon such a poor worm as I am, would I not go into His presence hoping against hope? Yet there is no *but* about it. *You cannot perish if you go.* We drink the medicine that the physician gives us in the hope that it may cure, but this *will* cure. Here is water that *will* quench your thirst. What a hammer those words "no wise" are with which to smash your fears to pieces. You cannot mention any shape or form of fear that these words do not slay upon the spot—"I will in no wise cast out." I wish I had an angel's tongue to declare the liberality of this. The devil may have given you twenty reasons against it, but take Jesus' word as enough.

There is also a great liberality in the text if you notice *its personality*. Jesus uses a large word in the first sentence: "*All* that the Father giveth me shall come." But in the second sentence, He uses a word that can mean *only one*, and He says, "him that cometh." There is personality here. It is not a massive group that He speaks to, but He invites us individually to come. The dying Savior died in our place as sinners. Is it hard for you to trust God who became man and so proved His love for you personally? Come to Him and you shall never be cast out. Your heaven is secure. You shall sit at the right hand of God and sing the new song of the white-robed saints. May the mighty Spirit come and make a difference as you look up at the Savior's cross. Looking there you shall never perish but willhave eternal life.